ALICE

Drawing of Alice Milligan by the Irish artist Seán
O'Sullivan (1906 - 1964). Pencil on paper, 1942.

ALICE

A Life of Alice Milligan

by

Sheila Turner Johnston

COLOURPOINT PRESS

COLOURPOINT PRESS
Omagh Business Complex
Gortrush
Omagh
Co Tyrone
BT78 5LS

ISBN 1 898392 01 3

© Sheila Johnston
   Omagh, 1994

The moral right of Sheila Johnston to be identified as the author of this work has been asserted.

This book has received support from the Cultural Traditions Programme of the Community Relations Council, which aims to encourage acceptance and understanding of cultural diversity.

Printed by The Northern Whig, Belfast

Illustrations: **Cover** - Portrait of Alice Milligan (1866 - 1953), painted 1918 by Estella F. Solomons (1882 - 1968). Photograph reproduced with the kind permission of the Trustees of the Ulster Museum.
Frontispiece - Alice Milligan drawn by Sean O'Sullivan in 1942. Courtesy of the National Gallery of Ireland.
All others, except page 28 - courtesy of the Milligan Estate.
Page 28 - courtesy of Methodist College, Belfast.

CONTENTS

To Norman, Wesley and Malcolm, with love

Also published by **Colourpoint Press**:

The Harper of the Only God: a selection of poetry by Alice Milligan. Edited by Sheila Turner Johnston, 1993.

Author's Preface

It is with trepidation that I see in print the results of some years of investigation into the life of Alice Milligan.

My interest in her was kindled on a purely personal level. Here was a woman who was born and who died in my own town. She was a Protestant who belonged not only to my own denomination but to my very own church society. And she was a Protestant who not only acknowledged her Irish identity but was gloriously proud to do so.

As I started my research, I thought I was going for a harmless paddle and ended having to do some energetic swimming! There is so much to appeal to us today in the life and work of this indomitable woman that I am amazed how unknown she has been until recently. I can only attribute this to the idea that the received view of history is the male view, for even in Omagh there is little knowledge of the importance of Alice Milligan in a critical period in Irish history.

My nervousness comes from the fact that I did not set out to produce an historical and academic treatise, and I have not. I fear however that there are some who will expect this and be critical. I hope that there will be many more who will simply enjoy, as I did, the unfolding story of a remarkable life.

This woman was attractive, stubborn, fascinating,

irritating, energetic yet vulnerable, and ultimately weakened by personal and political tragedy. I hope I have been just and true to her determined spirit in life. I also hope I have done some small service to her neglected shade.

My thanks to all those who encountered me during my research, and yet retained their patience. My particular appreciation goes to my husband who, unlike me, *is* an historian. At times he must think I married him because I needed a history reference book. I can assure him that this is not true — although he is indeed a very high-class publication.

Thanks also to Kate McAllister of the Irish and Local Studies Library here in Omagh, who tolerated my rummaging around and dealt with my weirder enquiries with tolerance and professionalism.

Sheila Johnston
Omagh, February 1994

Introduction

The interests and achievements of Alice Milligan's life were rooted in factors already bubbling in the Irish cauldron at the time of her birth in the 1860's.

Ireland had reached a decade of change. Socially and economically the country was at last beginning to put the devastation of the famine years behind it. There was a new confidence in the industrial potential of areas such as Belfast, which grew in prosperity as its linen industry expanded. Men like Seaton Milligan, Alice's father — and consequently Alice's family — were beneficiaries of this new industrial strength.

The railways were of enormous significance. Twenty years before, they were tentatively fingering Irish soil. By the 1860's they had spread to such an extent that they were a major factor in both personal and business life.

The time taken to transport goods between cities was cut in some cases to one fifth of its previous time. Towns formerly isolated in rural Ireland became linked by this cheap quick mode of transport. Remoteness became less of a disability as the major cities of Dublin, Belfast, Cork, Galway and Limerick became accessible by rail.

Many towns on the rail routes prospered as a result. Alice Milligan's birthplace, Omagh in Co Tyrone, was one of these. Omagh was linked by a through line to Belfast in 1861 and her father made full use of the rail network for his business interests.

The railways had an impact also on tourism. Taking a day at the seaside became a reality for the first time for a generation of Irish children. Wealthier families, like the Milligans, were able even to take houses for the whole summer at resorts like Bundoran in Co Donegal. The rail connection enabled them to keep the essential contact with home and business.

Although some time later, in the 1890's, another significant development worth noting in the world of transport was the arrival of the bicycle. This machine increased the independence of individuals who now had a virtually free mode of travel, limited only by their own energy. It had a part to play in the release of women from dependence on male dominated transport methods.

It is interesting also to wonder how much the success of an organisation such as the Gaelic League depended on the train and the bicycle. The message of Irish nationhood and independence was brought right to the heart of areas hitherto remote indeed. Alice Milligan celebrated the travelling teachers of the League in her poem 'The Man on the Wheel'.

Politically, the Fenian movement dominated the 1860's. Their ill-fated Rising took place in March 1867, before Alice was a year old. Its freshness in the minds of ordinary people is demonstrated in the nurse's warning to the Milligan children to:

Come in, or when it's dark
The Fenians will get ye! ('When I was a Little Girl')

However the Fenian movement was dead by the end of the decade and the new political movements which were to shape the last third were on the verge of emerging — the Home Rule movement under Parnell, the Gaelic Athletic Association, the Gaelic League and the intertwined Literary Revival.

Co-incidentally, the year of Alice's birth also saw an early debate on an issue which would come to dominate the minds of many Irish women for the next forty years and more. In 1866, John Stuart Mill presented to the House of Commons the first petition seeking female suffrage.

Although the Irish women's suffrage movement ran parallel to the English struggle, it faced difficulties unique to itself. Unlike their English sisters, the Irish suffragists were agitating for a vote to a Parliament they wished to remove from the government of their country. Inevitably this caused tensions as some Irish women put their nationalism before their suffragist beliefs. Some, such as Constance Markievicz, maintained a state of fervour for both, whilst for others — Alice Milligan among them — the cause of Irish independence admitted no rivals.

When I was a little girl
In a garden playing,
A thing was often said
To chide us, delaying

When after sunny hours,
At twilight's falling
Down through the garden walks
Came our old nurse calling -

"Come in! for it's growing late,
And the grass will wet ye!
Come in! or when it's dark
The Fenians will get ye!"

(from 'When I was a Little Girl')

1

The Little Girl

In Coalisland, Co Tyrone, some time before 1850, a young widow packed up her belongings and, with her little daughter beside her, travelled back to Omagh to nurse her grief and rear her child. She was returning to the farm from which she had been married only a few years previously. Her husband had been a Burns, a member of a family which had come over from Scotland in the 1690's and set up an earthenware and pottery business.

The marriage lasted only long enough for one daughter, Charlotte, to be born. Fatherless, the child nevertheless grew up happily with her mother and grandparents, enjoying the land, the lakes and the busy life of a flourishing farm, just outside the town.

In 1836, Mr. Kennedy Milligan of Glencar, Co Tyrone was presented with a son. He was named Seaton Forest. He was destined to go far in the world of business. In 1857, a raw 21 year old, he entered the firm of Hawkins, Robertson and Ferguson of Belfast who had started trading in 1852 in the Bank Buildings. This company was to become, in 1880, the better known Robertson, Ledlie and Ferguson Company, Ltd.

Seaton Milligan's brief was to open and develop the wholesale end of the business. This meant travelling the length and breadth of the country, particularly Ulster and Connaught, establishing contacts with suppliers, staying in hotels, using the railway where possible and horse transport for those areas the railway had not yet reached. He made the acquaintance of Charles Bianconi during the transport genius's declining years.

Seaton was often away for weeks at a time and did not occupy himself exclusively with business. During these years of travel he developed a great interest in and love for the Irish countryside and its history. This passion never left him, and was to be very fertile soil for his future family.

In the late 1850's the Ulster Railway from Belfast was open only as far as Portadown. The link to Dungannon and Omagh was under construction. Seaton Milligan, Commercial Traveller, well used to life on the road, often had occasion to stay in Omagh at the White Hart Hotel. This was a large building on the rising ground at the top of High Street. It was an important centre in the developing town and carriages came and went from its doors regularly.

On one such visit to the White Hart, Seaton met a young lady to whom he took more than a passing fancy. She, it seems, was equally smitten with this personable young businessman who had both intelligence and charm. Her name was Charlotte Burns.

They were married on 28th January 1862 in the Wesleyan Methodist Chapel in Omagh, which had been completed just a few years before, in 1857.

The young couple settled in Belfast and the first two of thirteen children were born there: Charlotte Olivia and Forest Boyd.

In the 1860's Belfast was not always a peaceful city and was shaken regularly by rioting of a sectarian and political nature. One of the favourite weapons of the mob was provided by the cobbled streets. Cobbles were prised out of the ground and one was dropped into the toe of a stocking. Whirled above the head, this made a very effective instrument.

Being a man of wide cultural tastes and acquainted as he was with the history and folklore of the countryside through which he travelled so frequently, Seaton Milligan's house contained many books, pictures and other evidence of his interests. In the hallway of the Milligan house was a picture of Robert Emmet.

One day Mrs. Milligan, now pregnant with her third child, returned home to find the house being attacked by rioters who were incensed by the picture in the hallway. One terrified maidservant was defending the house with the master's gun.

Charlotte, reared around tranquil blue lakes near Omagh, was distraught. She had two children to fear for and a baby soon to arrive. Belfast finally became too much for her.

Once again her Omagh relatives provided a haven. They brought Charlotte and her children back to Omagh and provided a cottage at Gortmore, just outside the town. There, on 14th September 1866, Alice Letitia was born.

Seaton Milligan was prospering and a cottage was not sufficient for his growing family. He acquiesced in the family remaining in Omagh and, with his own occupation of Commercial Traveller, a base in this growing town — his wife's home town — cannot have been too inconvenient. This was especially true as the railway connection between Belfast and Omagh had been opened in 1861.

Alice's mother, Charlotte Burns, about the time of her
marriage in 1862.

Mr. Milligan chose a new part of the town and built an impressive house at Campsie, just where the new road out of Omagh forked. On one side the road went to Mountfield and Cookstown and on the other, to Beragh, Carrickmore and Sixmilecross.

There, commanding a view down the length of Campsie Road, over the Drumragh River and into the town, stood — and still stands — the house which Seaton Milligan built for his family.

Many years later, about 1910, Alice accompanied her sister Charlotte when she returned to Omagh to collect and write down some Gaelic folk songs. Alice recalled:

Our car took the prettiest road out of Omagh, bringing me past the home of my childhood at the crossroads. There I saw the fir trees as tall as the church steeple which I had known when they were no higher than my head.

Alice's childhood in Omagh was happy and comfortable. Her family's lifestyle was typical of the well-to-do, upper crust Protestant elite. The Ascendancy cannot have known of the black sheep which grew quietly in its midst. Charlotte ran the house efficiently with the help of all the attendants which one would expect of a respected provincial family.

One of the most essential members of staff for the young Milligans was the nursemaid who presided over the fruitful nursery. When a new baby was expected, Alice and her brothers and sisters were dispatched to the farm where their mother had been reared. There they stayed until all was once again in order at home and Charlotte was well enough to oversee her increased family.

Social visits to her maternal grandmother's home, coupled with the longer stays during her mother's confinements, ensured that Alice spent a lot of time there and got to know the family well. She would wander around the lakes looking for duck eggs. She was particularly close to her great-uncle. Through him she gained childish experience of the hiring fairs where the farmers recruited their labourers.

At this time, the third quarter of the nineteenth century, many young men came from the West of Ireland to the hiring fairs in Strabane, Omagh and Newtownstewart looking for work. These were native Irish speakers and Alice's great-uncle carried out all his dealings in the hiring fairs and with his men on the farm, in the Irish language. Thus was a seed sown in the young Alice Milligan. She was active and adventurous and, probably more than the rest of her family, she was likely to accompany her great-uncle and hear the rhythms of the Irish speech used in everyday commerce.

Many years later she wrote a poem called 'A Harvester' about a young hired man she had met. The labourer is rather romanticised but Alice writes:

> And so it is I meet you here
> Binding the sheaves in mid-Tyrone,
> Hired in the farm along the lake,
> The farm my mother's kindred own.
>
> The light of joy is in your eyes,
> Gay was that snatch of music sung,

And checked to answer in surprise
My greeting in the Irish tongue.

Alice Milligan's literary abilities emerged early. The family was acquainted with Nathaniel Carson who was proprietor of one of the local papers, The Tyrone Constitution. Alice used to write out poems in a childish hand and give them to him, pleading with him to print them.

As she played in the garden of her home she could see the traffic on the roadways which passed on either side, making its way to and from the town. She remembered particularly watching the turf carts coming in from Mountfield. Turkeys were also bred in the area and Alice was scared of them. If she was out for a walk with her nurse she would plead "Don't go the turkey way!"

It was a happy family. Sometimes in the summer they would pack up a picnic and set out for a day in the Gortin Glens. They also stayed in Bundoran, Co Donegal, and many summer days were spent along the rocks by the sea. The rail link, opened the year Alice was born in June 1866, had opened up this part of Donegal to the tourist and traveller.

Next to Tyrone, Alice retained an abiding love for Donegal. About 1896 she wrote in *The Northern Patriot* (see page 82) that she was:

...a daughter of Tyrone, who knows and loves every mountain peak and headland of Red Hugh's country; from Inishowen and the waves of Swilly, round by lone Falcarragh and Gweedore, through the lake-sprinkled Rosses away on to Glencolmcille and southward over the fall of Assaroe, to the Drowse river; who has even stood where many a Donegal man has never stood, at the base of Columbcille's cross in remote Tory of the Formorians.

Alice did not start travelling for the Gaelic League until about 1906. This extract from *The Northern Patriot*, written ten years earlier, illustrates just how far her knowledge of her country had developed via mere personal and family exploration.

Alice's personality and interests owe a lot to her parents. Her father was intensely interested in the archaeology of the Irish countryside. He was elected a Member of the Royal Irish Academy in 1887 and became a Fellow in 1888. He contributed articles such as those to the Journal of the Royal Society of Antiquaries and gave lectures to societies and interest groups. He organised many archaeological expeditions around the coasts of the North. Some of the artifacts which he found on his travels were donated to the collections of the Royal Irish Academy. He had an extensive library which was at the disposal of his academically inclined daughter. It is likely that it was through her father's encouragement that Alice is able to boast in *The Northern Patriot* that, before she was thirty years old she had visited Tory Island.

Seaton Milligan does not appear to have been the archetypical Victorian father who sheltered his daughters from danger and cosseted them until a suitable husband could be found. Down the years also comes the distinct impression that Alice would not have tolerated being so treated.

Seaton made friends with this strong minded daughter and together they shared many common interests. They collaborated on a short tourist guide which they called *Glimpses of Erin*. This was published in 1888 when she was only twenty two.

Mr. Milligan showed a concern for the education and advancement of ordinary people and became associated with the Working Men's Institute, for whom he organised lectures. Alice paid tribute to him in these words: "As an historian he saw to it that we knew history and discussed with us children international affairs and literature".

This father was indeed far from being a stuffy Victorian. Although firmly of the Protestant tradition, he was expansive in his love of the country he lived and worked in. In those days — before polarisation became the mark of one's particular tribe — Seaton Milligan worked not only for the land but for the people who depended upon it. It was fertile soil and Alice's roots took hold and went very deep.

Seaton was also untypical in that he was as thoughtful for the education of his daughters as of his sons.

Alice started her education in Omagh at a private school run by Mrs. Knighton. Alice remembered her as being very ladylike and wearing her hair in a long thick plait which hung over one shoulder and reached to her waist.

Seaton's considerate treatment of his daughters may owe something to the regard in which he held his wife. One of the steadiest influences upon Alice was the happy marriage of her parents. The feelings kindled by the first meeting in the White Hart Hotel in Omagh, matured and settled into a devotion which lasted for over fifty years.

Charlotte Burns bore thirteen children and out-

Alice's father, Seaton Forest Milligan.

lived four of them. While the family was still resident in Omagh she lost two of her sons. In 1873 little Frederick George died in Bundoran while still a baby. On the surround of the Milligan grave near Omagh are the simple words "George, died in infancy". In 1875 in a terrible blow the Milligan's second child and eldest son, Forest Boyd, died at the age of ten.

Charlotte was an active and optimistic lady and although these sorrows were bitter and heavy she rallied for the sake of her other children. Alice had a good relationship with her and all the family held her in great affection.

Ernest Milligan, the second last child, published a small volume of poetry called *Up Bye Ballads* under the pseudonym of Will Carew. In it there is a poem called 'The Voice by the Fire'. The speaker is not necessarily the poet, but the image must be drawn from some memory:

> When sittin' lonely by the fire, me thoughts 'll
> oftimes go
> To childhood days an' memories dear in time
> of long ago;
> Once more a little child I am aside me mother's
> knee,
> An' soft an' low her voice I hear as she would
> sing to me.
>
> .... in the firelight glow I see her face so bright
> An' tender with the look of love that she still
> smiled on me.

Perhaps one of the most revealing insights into

Mrs. Milligan's character and a sign of how she was regarded by friends, is provided by a very famous murder which occurred during the Milligan's time in Omagh.

In 1871, Mr. Glass, bank cashier in Newtown-stewart, Co Tyrone, was brutally murdered while at his desk. Thomas Hartley Montgomery was the highly esteemed District Inspector of Police who at once started an investigation. However, very shortly it transpired that Montgomery, who had been a friend of Mr. Glass, was in fact, the murderer. The whole of Victorian Britain took an interest in this case and for a while West Tyrone was in the spotlight as Montgomery was taken to reside in Omagh Gaol. Attempts at appeal failed. The wheels of the law turned slowly. The night of 25th August 1873 was wild and stormy. At dawn on the 26th Thomas Hartley Montgomery was executed by hanging.

Upper class society in Omagh had been stunned. In most houses Montgomery had been a welcome visitor. To realise the true nature of the man whom they had entertained and who had played with their children, sent them into a state of shock.

The execution took place in the summer and many families had left for the seaside. On the day of the execution any remaining prominent families left the town. The Milligan's were in Bundoran. It was the duty of the Church of Ireland minister, Reverend Charters, Chaplain to the prison, to attend Montgomery on his way to execution.

Charters was extremely upset by this task. As soon as the formalities were completed after the hanging he jumped on the next train to Bundoran and arrived at Mrs. Milligan's door. Alice always remembered her mother's concern for the minister. Charlotte made up a couch for him to lie on and he rested with them until he felt able to return. This was in August, and Charlotte had lost her little son George only the previous April.

Such was Alice Milligan's home base: parents who loved her and who cared for her intellect as well as her body; parents who were highly regarded in the community and who provided a comfortable prosperous existence; a family life which was active and filled with curiosity; and an environment which encouraged literary inclinations where-ever they showed themselves.

Alice always traced her political awareness back to her childhood in Omagh. She told of learning to ride on a shaggy pony on the roads around her home. One day she was accompanied by a hired boy called Roddy, who, in her own words, was "a native Irishman ... a veritable Rory of the Hills. As we went along he discoursed treason in fascinating style". They came across the words "Home Rule For Ireland" painted on a wall alongside a drawing of a harp which was not surmounted, as was usual, with a crown. Roddy apparently was only too happy to explain and elaborate. Alice, still a child, was fascinated. She began to note the names of Isaac Butt and Parnell in the newspapers. Her young inquisitive mind noticed when the harp was erased, the inscription was altered to "No Home Rule" and "very rude remarks were added about his Holiness the Pope".

It may have been that same outing or another, when the boy accompanying her on her pony met up with a friend. The two boys sat on the grass by the roadside and talked about the current political happenings. Alice dismounted and sat patiently on the grass a little apart, listening. She did not recall the whole conversation, but remembered one boy saying to the other as they stood to part: "Ah well, we'll see what this new man Parnell does".

Alice's poem 'When I Was A Little Girl' is a delightful account of her Omagh childhood and highlights her own early sense of seeing things differently from those around her; of being a child of a tangled web of ancestry which had placed her into a privileged tradition but, while doing so, had given her the freedom and security to rebel if she choose.

In the late 1870's Seaton Milligan became a director of the Bank Buildings. His days as a commercial traveller were at an end. A return to Belfast was unavoidable. The family packed up and said goodbye to Omagh. In November 1878 the family home was sold to representatives of St. Columba's Parish Church, and it became a Rectory.

For Alice there followed a period of quiescence, Nothing was forgotten but much had yet to be learnt before a mature woman could stand out on her own and defend her particular political certainties.

2

The Wild Flower

The family moved into No. 1 Royal Terrace on the Lisburn Road in Belfast. This terrace was demolished in the 1970's. The Milligans needed a large house and at Royal Terrace there was ample accommodation.

It was one of a tall Victorian terrace of houses which rose from the kitchens in the basement to the attics above the nursery. The nursery was on the third floor and ran the full width of the house. This was the territory of 'Old Jane'.

Jane was remembered by Alice and by all who knew her as one of life's characters. She had served in the household of Mary Ann McCracken, sister of Henry Joy, and when her mistress died the year Alice was born, Jane had obtained a position with the Milligans. She lived to a great age and the family ensured her comfort until she died.

As often happened in such circumstances, she became much more than a servant, and shared out her quick tongue, her rough and ready cooking and her total devotion in generous measures.

A distinguished clergyman is reputed to have called at the house one day. The Milligans' dog barked most threateningly and Jane opened the door a crack:

"You may be the Dean of Down, but the dog thinks you're the postman!" she called — and closed the door.

Alice's school photograph, taken at the Methodist College, Belfast.

Fortunately, the Dean had a sense of humour.

The family were at least fifteen years in Royal Terrace, and the last child, Charles, was born there in 1888. During these years many influences surrounded Alice.

She became more aware of social conditions outside her own privileged surroundings. The Milligan house was opposite the Workhouse gates and from the windows of her home Alice and her brothers and sisters could watch the Workhouse children leaving and returning at regular intervals as they went out to school.

Alice was sent to the Methodist College in 1879. This was a comparatively new school having been opened only eleven years before. It was also just down the road from home and the walk to school and back every day become very familiar.

The years of Alice's secondary schooling marched alongside the further development of the Irish women's suffrage movement. Three years before Alice went to the Methodist College, the Youghal Quaker, Anna Haslam, had formed the Irish Women's Suffrage and Local Government Association in Dublin.

These beginnings do not appear to have impinged on the schoolgirl or her family. They were busy and fulfilled and Alice did not feel personally and deeply at this stage that she was denied anything which should have been hers by right.

Indeed, in education, doors opened for her with the passing of the Intermediate Education Act in 1878, just the year before she began her secondary schooling. Alice and her contemporaries were now able to compete on equal terms with their male classmates in the Intermediate examinations. Typically Alice rose to the challenge and won a medal in these examinations.

Nowhere does she say that her schooldays were unhappy. She possessed a nature which seized each new situation and shook it dry of experience. So at the Methodist College she cemented her inborn aptitudes into a deep foundation of academic knowledge.

Later her interest was to narrow almost obsessively to all things Irish. Ireland— legendary, political, cultural— was the great theme of her life. During her teenage years and early twenties, this preoccupation, though present, was not yet dominant. She was attempting to learn Irish through the little primers which were available, but through her family and her own education she had a broad knowledge from which to make the informed choice of her own special sphere. At the back of one of her diaries she has made notes on the works of Shakespeare, Spencer, Jonson and many others. Occasionally, as when Tennyson died, she allowed herself to be sidetracked into quite lengthy literary criticisms. She carefully notes the deaths of Browning and Whitman.

However, she did later lament the lack of Irish awareness in her schooling. In her autobiographical 'Ode for 6th October' (the date of the death of Charles Stewart Parnell) she recalls a childhood devoid of the legends of her native country:

> Ireland dear! through the length of my childhood lonely,
> Throughout the toilsome hours of my schooling days,
> No mention of thee was made unto me, save only
> By speakers in heedless scorn or in harsh dispraise.

Despite this deprivation she declares:

> As a wild flower out of seed of God's own sowing
> Grew in my heart this flower of my love for thee.

She was not always a model pupil. Early on there are signs of her ability as a ring leader.

Her Classics master was Mr. J.G. Meyer, M.A. and he was well known amongst his students as being a master of the art of digression. He would announce the subject matter of the lesson to his pupils, but within minutes had wandered unrecognisably from the topic.   If challenged, he would pause, and then meticulously retrace his steps of digression back to the starting point and announce triumphantly "You see. It arose out of the lesson!"

On one occasion Alice organised a rebellion amongst her classmates and stopped his every attempt to leave the subject in hand. Eventually she provoked his wrath and he denounced her as a rebel and obstructionist and one of the wickedest and most disagreeable people he had ever taught. He could recall having taught only one more wicked person. When he was at Trinity College, Dublin, he had given extra tuition to a youth called Charles Stewart Parnell — " the man " he said fiercely, "who is trying to wreck the British Empire."

In later years the memory of having once been a runner-up to Parnell — albeit in wickedness — gave Alice great satisfaction.

Nevertheless, she excelled at school, showing an aptitude which ranged across the curriculum. Her prizes included, in 1882 Music Theory, 1883 Maths, English and Scripture and in 1884 Science and the Senior Grade Book Prize. She was also a keen sketcher and her quick pen drawings enliven her diaries. She matriculated in 1886.

Her school photograph shows a pretty and alert young girl, head resting on one hand in a pose to be repeated throughout her life. Her hair, which was of flaming red, flows down her back. Her gaze at the camera is very straight and open; her manner conveys a lively intelligence.

Throughout her schooldays she continued to write

poetry. One of her first poems ever to be circulated, 'The River', appeared in a manuscript school magazine called *Eos*. In fact this magazine gave her her first audience of any size. 'A Suggestion to Political Tourists', which was included in *Glimpses of Erin*, first appeared here, as did 'Credo et Dubitas'.

Her father was continuing to make his own mark. In 1884 he was elected to Membership of the Royal Society of Antiquaries of Ireland and in 1887 he became a Member of the Royal Irish Academy.

Life was very pleasant for the young family. They were a closely knit unit which nevertheless was expansive in its friendships and activities. The friends of both parents and children were welcome in the house and overnight visitors were commonplace. Picnics were a favourite pastime.

A seaside residence was a social necessity for such a family. In Omagh the Milligans had escaped to Bundoran for the summer. Now they made their way to the Co Down coast. Their first holiday home was a cottage in Donaghadee called Angus' Cottage. If the weather was favourable, Mama (with the accent on the last syllable) Milligan closed up Royal Terrace at Easter and the family stayed at the coast until about Hallowe'en. The railway made such migrations possible. Seaton Milligan was able to travel to work at the Bank Buildings every day, summer and winter, where-ever the family headquarters happened to be. All the family were habitual travellers hither and thither. Alice loved to travel and wrote of hopping on trams and racing for the train.

She was quite intrepid and thought nothing of

long journeys alone. On one occasion, still in her early twenties, she visited friends in Cushendall. Her return journey as far as Larne was made on an old Bianconi - style long car. Her neighbour on the long car was a sailor en route to Belfast to join a ship. Initially the sailor's company was beyond reproach. However, the longcar stopped every so often to pick up passengers and refresh the horses. Meanwhile the sailor refreshed himself at any nearby public house.

By the time the long car arrived at Carnlough the driver had observed that Alice's situation was becoming difficult.

While the sailor was indoors having another drink, a quick swap was done with a gentleman from the other side of the long car.

The sailor hopped on just as the car moved off. After a few seconds he started a fuss : "Stop! You've left behind that wee red-headed girl!"

On the far side, Alice kept her head down and the driver took no notice. The sailor changed tack and from there to Larne hurled abuse at the bad, bad driver who had left behind a wee red-headed girl in Carnlough.

The last stage of the journey was by train to Belfast. Alice managed to be alone on the train but encountered the sailor on the platform in Belfast. She hurried past and he never did find out how she got from Carnlough to Belfast.

Alice's sisters were sent to complete their education in Germany. When Alice matriculated she went no further than the Ladies Department of King's College, London, where she attended lectures in English Literature and English History. University records furnish the mere fact of her attendance and give no clue to her personal achievements or activities. However, there is one poem, 'In Exile', which is from her early days and could well voice her state of mind as a twenty year old home-loving Ulsterwoman in London:

> Dying you say! I long to die;
> My soul is tired of earth -
> Of the weary day and the weary night
> When all regrets have birth;
> My sight is sick of that poplar tree
> Where the sparrows perch and flit,
> Of the dreary stretch of the whitewashed wall,
> The blue sky over it.

Whatever the reason, the summer of 1887 saw her home again. Her family and friends were very important to her. Her independent mind ranged freely but emotionally she formed deep attachments, some of which were to cause her great grief. Of her sisters she was closest to the eldest of the family, Charlotte.

Charlotte was very gifted musically and from an early age her path in the world of music was clear. Her father sent her to the Conservatoire in Frankfurt, and she returned to London to the Royal College of Music. Probably at this time she met the solicitor, Fox, who later became her husband. Before marriage, however, Charlotte returned to Europe to the Milan Conservatoire.

Alice missed her. Charlotte was a companion of

the old Omagh days in a way the younger siblings were not. At Christmas in 1882 Alice, still a school-girl, records that she received a "box from Cha."

Charlotte later went on to become well known as Charlotte Milligan-Fox. In 1904 she founded the Irish Folk Song Society. She wrote original songs as well as researching and recording, in manuscript form, native Gaelic folk songs.

This work took her to remote country areas to meet the singers. Alice sometimes accompanied her. Charlotte's *Annals of the Irish Harpers* of 1911 is a classic work, the result of her research gathering and editing Edward Bunting's collection of Irish music for the harp.

News of her work spread to the United States where she was invited to undertake a lecture tour. After her marriage she settled in London where her house became a meeting place for musical and liter-ary figures.

Of her brothers Alice was fiercely attached to Seaton. Since the death of Forest Boyd in 1875 in Bundoran, Seaton Kennedy Milligan was the eldest son, although fifth in the family and three years younger than Alice. Seaton returned the affection, and amongst a large and lively circle of friends these two remained kindred spirits and mutual confidantes. Habitually they went for walks together when they shared thoughts and dreams of the years to come.

She had many friends of both sexes and a picture emerges of an intelligent and fun loving young woman who had a quick wit, a quick tongue and a vivid enjoyment of all life had to offer.

Her flame-haired presence was popular and sought

after. Nevertheless, within herself Alice was searching for an aim and a meaning to her life. The gnawing germ of loneliness and nonfulfillment was as yet young, but one day it would clamour for response.

She was still writing. 'An Idyll of the Red City' describes Belfast and its mills coming awake. Sonnets like 'On the Cliff' and 'A Winter's Night Reverie' illustrate her relationship with her surroundings.

The first few lines of the latter sonnet are evocative:

> I love the quiet of my room to gain
> On some wild night of winter storms and stars
> That fly as sparks from out the furnace bars.

In the autumn of 1887 Alice went to Derry to take up a post as a governess at the Ladies' Collegiate School run by the Misses MacKillip. There were two other governesses with whom she made friends. Mademoiselle Cazalong taught French and Alice nicknamed her 'La Marsellaise'. In return Mademoiselle referred to Alice as 'Meeligano'.

The other governess was the young music teacher, Marjorie Arthur who was also Alice's room-mate. Alice referred to her as 'The Highland Lassie' because she was from Scotland. Her mother's people were MacDonalds from Skye.

Throughout her life Alice never suffered fools gladly. Conversely, when she gave loyalty to a cause or a person her devotion was absolute.

Alice found in Marjorie Arthur a friend who was the perfect foil for her vivid personality. Both were fun-loving and full of laughter. But Marjorie was also gentle and serene, where Alice was impelled by a more aggressive spirit. This deep friendship, through tragedy, was to be the genesis of some of Alice's finest verse.

This was in the future. The academic year 1887 - 88 was a happy year for La Marsellaise, The Highland Lassie and Meeligano. Alice was the only one who was in her native land and she became an unofficial guide to the countryside around. She was free at a certain time each week, whereas the other two had to alternate school duties on a two week rota.

Thus one week Mademoiselle would appear before her and stamp her foot. Years later Alice could still recall her voice: "Meeligano! put down zat seely newspaper deer - r - r -rectly. It is only on von day in ze fortnight I ask you to valk vid me. Sacre au nom d'un chien! It vill be dark at five o'clock. Bring me somefare today!"

So Alice would take her perhaps to Corrody Hill to look down on Derry City which, she said over ten years later: "appeared under a frosty sky, with the wide Foyle flowing around it ... Far away on the horizon's edge, where the sky was scarlet, stood a line of mountains blue as sapphire, and the red river seemed to come like a fiery serpent all the way from there to the walls of Derry".

Alice loved such scenery and was able to describe vividly many parts of Ireland seen in different moods, especially Donegal. Proudly she showed her two friends Lough Swilly, Glendermot, Aonach Lough, Culmore Ferry, Prehen Wood and - one of her favourite places - the Grianan of Aileach.

When she went to Corrody with Marjorie the weather was never in their favour. One evening Alice grew quite annoyed when, straining her eyes through the mist, she spotted dimly Errigle and Barnesmore. Her ecstasy at this was such that Marjorie sat on the rocks and laughed heartily, telling her that she should see the Highland hills!

Marjorie was rather homesick and from Corrody she could see the steamers swinging out on their way to Scotland, and many times she wished she was going with them.

Alice's boundless energy was a feature which her pupils remembered. She discovered that many of the girls had never seen the sunrise. With permission, she set about providing this part of their education:

And so it comes that my memory of school life includes pictures of Marjorie and myself and that devoted band walking on the hill crests before dawn waiting to see the sun come up and the mists rolling away from the hills above Derryrider.

She had a great desire to show Lough Swilly to Marjorie on a fine day. She never managed it but vivid always in her memory was the day she nearly succeeded. Looking out of their high window one day she discovered that she could see as far as the cliffs of Inishowen and thought idly what a view there would be from Aileach today! Typically, on the heels of the thought came action. She called to Marjorie to put on her Tam-o-Shanter for they were going for a long drive to the Grianan of Aileach and when they came back she would never laugh at the

Donegal hills again.

Marjorie tried to discourage her, saying that it would be selfish to take a car just for two. Why not wait until St. Patrick's Day when a group could be organised? Alice would not be dissuaded, even when she had to borrow the fare from a rather reluctant colleague, promising a refund on pay day.

It was a long winding drive for the carriage and, as they travelled, the mountain mist came down. Marjorie, who knew all about mountain mists, tentatively doubted that they would see anything. Alice would have none of it and even when they were scrambling up the last part of the hill on foot, in the middle of a cold grey mist, wet to the knees from the heather, she was cheerfully hoping that it might be clear on the other side. She stopped at a certain point and declared "It is just at this point that the view bursts upon you"!

"I see nothing but mist, "said the pragmatic Marjorie, "and if you don't take care you'll walk over a precipice".

They stood together shivering and Alice assured her that they were face to face with the finest view in the whole world.

They could not even see the fort. Marjorie commented astutely: "It's an adventure anyhow, and you are always looking for adventures".

The mist thinned briefly and they saw the doorway of the Grianan not six feet from them. Even now Alice did not give up, and with Marjorie holding on to her skirts, she groped along, found some steps and precariously mounted to the top of the circular wall. Into the grey curtain she renewed her description of the view and the history of the fort. Again Marjorie had to laugh until the walls echoed with it, and again Alice felt vexation.

They had difficulty finding the door again and even greater difficulty finding their carriage. Dusk had fallen on the long journey home. They had one fur boa between them and they wound it round them both against the cold. Alice's disappointment was keener than Marjorie's for Alice had been to Aileach before and knew that what she had tried to share was indeed beautiful. Looking back at Aileach they discovered that the sky was clear from east to west, with stars beginning to wink in the darkness.

Several weeks later when Alice was in Dublin, Marjorie Arthur went to Lough Swilly and walked along the shore at Faughan. She climbed to the top of a high hill and at last saw the hills of Donegal. She wrote to Alice: "It is as beautiful as the Highlands".

Shadows of these days haunt the best poetry Alice Milligan ever wrote.

In February 1888 her great uncle died in Omagh at the age of 79 having survived his wife by two years. The Milligan family kept alive their connections with the Omagh farm— it was, after all, Mrs. Milligan's home. Irish continued to be spoken on the farm for many years as the labourers and maids were hired from The Rosses, a Gaelic speaking region in Donegal. Arguably, with the going of her great-uncle went also the person responsible for Alice's love of the Irish language and her eventual direction in life.

During 1888 Alice's father was made a Fellow of the Royal Society of Antiquaries of Ireland, and baby Charles was born. Twenty-four years separated the eldest child from the youngest and Alice was twenty-two when her last brother arrived. It was not until her middle age that she really began to know Charles. To the young woman he was just 'Baby' and rather a nuisance. When entertaining 'Mr. Yeates' she complained:

We ... sat in the library where the conversation was perpetually interrupted by Baby and the two black cats with occasional interruptions from the terrible pup ...

Yeats appears to have endured Baby, cats and pup with fortitude for the conversation was a long one.

The Milligan parents still hoped that this particular daughter would obediently follow her sisters and develop her musical talents on the Continent. This was a most suitable course for a young lady in her position.

But Alice did not want to go. She did not see her pathway lying in that direction. Her independent mind stood out once more and she requested permission to go to Dublin to learn the Irish language. We do not know if there was a battle of wills over this. Perhaps not. The distance between the thinking of father and daughter was not great. Seaton had written in *Glimpses of Erin*:

Patriotism ... far from being an irrational sentiment is entirely rational and desirable from a utilitarian point of view. It is as much so from a Christian standpoint. By living in our own land and doing our best to benefit it, we can best carry out the command 'Do unto others as you would that they should do unto you'.

Late in the year 1888 Alice pencilled in her diary: "I off to Dublin". This decision precipitated the most formative period of her entire life.

3

The Headlong Spirit

In living for three years in the Irish capital, Alice brought herself into the stimulating air of undiluted nationalism. For the first time, without the distraction of family opinions, social affairs and expectations, she came into 'Irish Ireland' and found at last the soul mate of her existence.

The soil had already been tilled. Clearly she loved the physical country enough to have no wish to finish her education on the continent. Politically the 1880's were eventful years and she followed with interest the fortunes of Parnell and Davitt in their fight for Home Rule and the activities of the Land League. She would have been aware of the growing rural revolt against landlordism stimulated by the mounting numbers of evictions which were instilling new strength into the Home Rule Movement and militant nationalism. At the Milligan home there would have been talk of 'Captain Moonlight' and his stealthy and uncompromising revenge on the perpetrators of agrarian injustice.

In 1886, when Gladstone's First Home Bill was defeated, Alice Milligan had just left school. Her brief - possibly unhappy - sojourn in London to study at King's College only served to reinforce her attachment to Ireland and particularly to Ulster.

By 1888 Alice was intellectually an Irishwoman. Ireland was in her head. The years in Dublin carved it on her heart.

In another sense also, the timing of Alice's awakening to Irish Ireland was critical. In London at the time lived a young poet by the name of William Butler Yeats, who was just one year older than Alice. He had just met Maud Gonne when, as he was to say later, "all the trouble of my life began". John O'Leary and Standish O'Grady had exerted their influence to make him write always and only about and for Ireland. George Russell (A.E.) was already a friend and had provoked an interest in mysticism.

In 1891 Yeats founded the Irish Literary Society in London and the next year he and John O'Leary founded the National Literary Society in Dublin.

Just at the beginning of this period, against a background of intense political activity, under the near kingship of Parnell, Alice Milligan arrived in Dublin. The constraints of family and Northern Protestantism were gone. She was free to think as she chose and to witness at first hand some events in the making of a nation.

Outwardly she was the pretty and intelligent daughter of a wealthy businessman. Underneath was the sensitive poetess searching for direction.

Within the next few years political inclination and literary ability were to fuse in a matrix uniquely suited to her particular genius.

She lodged in rooms in Merrion Square near the centre of Dublin and not far from Trinity College. She studied widely in the Royal Irish Academy and the National Library in Kildare Street. Although ostensibly she had come to Dublin to learn the Irish language she did not confine her explorations and so expanded further her already extensive literary and artistic knowledge.

She became part of an intellectual but easy-going group of friends who delighted to call upon each other, and to promenade round Stephen's Green and along what was becoming known as O'Connell Street.

She had female friends but male company was also easy to find. In May 1891 she describes in her diary a delightful afternoon verbally sparring with a young man called Uther. They discussed the teaching profession, visited the library and "criticised the busts. Aristotle fine, Burke very poor". They went round Trinity College chapel and exam hall — "decided that the name porphyry was too good for the substance as exampled in a monument there".

The two then adjourned to Uther's room in Trinity College for afternoon tea. It would be another 13 years before she could as a woman have joined him as a student at Trinity. Her diary makes no reference to this prohibition. They discussed Rembrandt and Shakespeare and "We agreed that America was uninhabitable— and that it is a place to go with the idea of returning".

This particular companion was youthfully opinionated. He did not like the English people and "he has a deep rooted scorn for the inhabitants of Belfast and laughed at their idea of Dublin as a deserted city".

About her relationships with the young men of her acquaintance, Alice is never explicit. She merely says of the end of her afternoon with Uther "we walked as far as the library together and then— adieu".

Such were the company and the opinions which

circulated around her now. She found a rapport with Dublin which she never found with London. Her stay was punctuated by visits to relatives in Omagh, to Marjorie in Derry and home to Belfast.

In relationships she had a self confidence which bears witness to her secure background and innate sense of her own worth. She was never a mistress of the art of self-effacement. And so it is in character when she manages to visit Michael Davitt, who had founded the Land League in 1879. Through her father she was already acquainted with the Davitts.

Alice's drawing of
Michael Davitt

When she heard that they were to leave Ireland shortly, she immediately penned a letter bidding them goodbye. She was rewarded by an invitation to visit them in Killiney, Dublin. She went by train and overtook Davitt just outside the station. He had lost an arm at the age of eleven and was carrying parcels, all tied together, in his remaining hand.

Alice introduced herself and spent a long afternoon with the family, having no difficulty at all in responding to Michael Davitt's topics of conversation.   Her wish to learn Irish was given encouragement.   Davitt told her that his mother, an ardent nationalist, had made all her children speak Irish, even in England. "To speak English," she said, "is a sign of servitude", and she would not give them anything that they could not ask for in Irish.

Davitt reminisced at length about his travels in Italy and the Holy Land, returning to the Irish question to lament that "this wretched political question" was keeping the country from settling down to industry.

He was totally relaxed in Alice's company, bringing in his children to sit on his knee and frowning out at the thrushes on his lawn as he expressed a desire to exterminate the whole race of cats. Alice was able to make him laugh heartily at some of her own stories and when she left he escorted her to the gate in the pouring rain. He gave her a warm invitation to visit them again on their return from America and to pick as many roses as she liked from his garden.

Alice's personality was a warm and attractive one. Years later the wife of O'Donovan Rossa wrote to her:

(We) have taken a very great liking to you ... One of those beneficent impulses may seize your headlong spirit to dive through Cork on your way to the North, and if so, oh please let us know, that we may warm ourselves in your sunny atmosphere more speedily. I'm going to make Rossa laugh reading this letter to him ...

The high point of her time in Dublin was her

attendance at a Parnell meeting in Inchicore. Every letter she received from Marjorie, who was still teaching in Derry, posed the question "Have you seen Parnell yet?" She had made several attempts but did not succeed until June 1891.

Parnell had, only six months before, suffered what is arguably one of the most tragic setbacks to a magnificent career which political history can provide. His long-standing affair with a married woman, Katherine O'Shea, was dragged into the open when Mrs. O'Shea's husband sued for divorce, citing Parnell as co-respondent. The liaison had lasted for ten years and was by no means casual. They had three children in the early 1880's and married as soon as Mrs. O'Shea was free.

The effect of the revelation, in late 1890, was catastrophic. Personally, Parnell never recovered from the humiliation. Politically the Home Rule cause was set back years. Gladstone said later: "I do believe firmly that if these divorce proceedings had not taken place there would be a Parliament in Ireland today". As it was, Gladstone felt he had to ask Parnell to resign as leader of the Irish Party. Parnell refused to go, accusing the Liberals of unacceptable interference in the affairs of another party.

Because of the nature of his offence the Catholic hierarchy, previously an ardent and influential supporter, now withdrew its blessing. This was an act which Alice Milligan never forgave and harked back to with bitterness in poetry and prose. The following lines are from 'Bonnie Charlie':

He trusted you as Irishmen,
Trusted and served you rarely,
Toiled to break your slavery's chain—
But ye were false to Charlie!

It seemed that the leader of Ireland's moral crusade had failed a morality test.

There was nevertheless a groundswell of popular support remaining. Alice, who was in Dublin when the scandal broke, found that her feelings were ambivalent. She teased Marjorie (who was Scottish) that her interest in Parnell was provoked only because his names were Charles Stewart! She had a very Alice-like impulse while sitting in a tram in Sackville Street: "I turned into a Parnellite. The conversion was sudden and most unaccountable—perhaps it won't last".

On a Sunday evening in May 1891 she heard that he was going to pass through Harcourt Street Station on his way to Wicklow. She stood for an hour beside a pillar at the entrance to the station, trembling with excitement and a little in fear of the large crowd which had assembled with the same hope of seeing "The Chief". She thought them largely disreputable looking and she always retained a nervousness of being in such company.

Even now she had great reservations and attached great importance to actually seeing Parnell. "If I had seen his face" she had written, "I would know whether to trust him".

She took the view that Parnell was right in insisting on the Irish Party's control of its own affairs but feared— rightly as it turned out— that he was acting

Sunday June-7.

Went with Miss E. Lilley to
Inchichore tram — & as we waited
in it a waggonette passed —
There-between Grattans
statue & the old parliament
house I saw for the
1st time in my life —
Parnell —
sitting beside Dr Kenny, sad
& silent — So pathetic looking.
Near Kilmainham we overtook
the waggonette which was blocked
in the midst of an admiring
crowd — There — I stood
up on the tram steps waving
my kerchief wildly excited
Dr Kenny plucked him
by the coat — (he wore a light

Alice's diary entry for June 7th 1891
"There between Grattan's statue and the old parliament house
I saw for the first time in my life — Parnell — sitting beside
Dr. Kenny sad and silent — so pathetic looking."

The opening page of one of Alice's diaries on which she has
sketched Parnell as she saw him in Dublin on June 7th 1891,
just months before his death.

like Samson. He would pull down the edifice and destroy himself, friends and enemies alike. He was, she thought, an impossible leader now, and he should withdraw for a while and hand the reins over temporarily. People would forgive and forget if given time.

Her vigil at Harcourt Street was in vain. Parnell did not come.

To her delirious excitement, she got her wish a week later. A Parnell meeting was held at Inchicore on 7th June 1891. With a friend she set off on the tram. While in the tram a wagonette passed them. Closer inspection identified the occupants:

There between Grattan's statue and the old parliament house I saw for the first time in my life— Parnell.

Her diary descriptions of the man as he now was are poignant. He was "sad and silent— so pathetic looking".

At Kilmainham, traffic was slowed and sometimes blocked by the huge crowds. The tram caught up with the wagonette again. Alice could sit still no longer and jumped up and down on the tram steps, waving her handkerchief. Inconspicuous observation was not her way. Parnell's companion, Dr. Kenny, drew his attention to the wildly excited girl on top of the tram. Parnell raised his hat to her.

But in the midst of her elation, Alice was shocked by his appearance. Later, in quietness, she wrote:

I will never forget the sad downcast expression — half

ashamed as it were, the ghastly pallor of his face— his dark eyes—rather shifty ... He looked beaten and ashamed.

The meeting was an occasion of high excitement for the seething crowd. Alice's dislike of such uncontrolled occasions intensified into actual fear as she and her friend were crushed and shoved in a pulsating throng of horses and — in her own words— "dirty people". Alice had her purse stolen. Its contents were typical of the owner — a ha'penny stamp and a pen nib.

The intrepid pair fought on and Alice compensated for her small stature by rising on tiptoe and exclaiming whenever she caught a glimpse of Parnell.

Parnell appears to have shaken off his melancholy when he found a platform under his feet. He displayed defiance and although rather hoarse and tired he stood tall and splendid with his arms folded. He smiled at the crowd and Alice sensed that there was hardly one who did not love him. She heard one comment "Look at him. Standin' up there smilin', not a bit ashamed — and why should he be?"

When Parnell descended from the platform the crowd rushed towards him and Alice was elbowed violently backwards. She recovered and this time waved her handkerchief so enthusiastically that she lost it altogether.

Parnell's progress was slow as hands were thrust out for him to shake. He shook all he could reach, a tired smile on his face.

Alice and her companion collapsed exhausted under a tree to rest. They had been standing for hours.

With difficulty Parnell's wagonette made its way to him and he mounted still surrounded on all sides. Marching bands contributed to the din with patriotic abandon.

After reaching down to touch more hands Parnell donned his coat, helped by Dr. Kenny and again Alice was struck by his appearance: "He was wretchedly thin — his collar bone showing through the coat". As the carriage lurched he almost fell, but recovered and remained standing as he was driven off, acknowledging the cheers by waving his hat. He had said: "I rely on Dublin. Dublin is true". So it seemed.

At last Alice saw him sit down wearily and disappear from sight. She wrote of the moment: "I had seen the last of Parnell".

Indeed she had. Four months later he was dead.

For Alice it had been a conversion experience which unsettled her to the core. She walked the streets of Dublin, restless and emotional, for days afterwards.

Less than three weeks after the Inchicore rally Parnell married Kitty O'Shea in Brighton.

Even before the Parnells were married, Alice had completed her course of study in Dublin. She returned to total relaxation at home.

Her Dublin experiences gave her a political nucleus and the evidence of that was to show itself very soon. After all, this red-headed young woman could boast that Michael Davitt had offered her roses and Charles Stewart Parnell had raised his hat to her.

4

Fear and Fame

Upsets and tragedies, both national and personal, occurred in the next few years to mar what was otherwise a very happy and carefree time with family and friends.

Increasingly as the years went by, the family spent more of the year at Bangor (which became their permanent east coast base) and less at Royal Terrace. Bangor in the 1890's was just beginning its growth and was still quite a small close knit community. The Milligan house was usually a bustle of friends and relations, coming, going and staying, the whole mix being liberally sprinkled with cats, kittens and the odd pup.

Just after Alice's return from Dublin several of her friends came to stay, including Mmlle. Cazalong and Marjorie Arthur from Derry. Other Omagh friends came for quite long visits. Mr. and Mrs. Milligan tolerated a house of quite informal freedom.

The rest of the family also brought friends. Alice's eldest sister Charlotte had made friends in London and one of these was Edith White. Alice did not like Edith and teased her mercilessly. We see here a glimpse of another side of Alice — where she disliked she was also rather intolerant. Edith took a great liking to Alice's brother Seaton. Perhaps this was a factor in Alice's dislike of her, although she never feared that her beloved brother would return Edith's affection. On the 13th August 1891, she reports disdainfully:

E White suddenly determined to go home, and furiously attacked the white and yellow cushion - I went to bed.

There was a little jetty near Hamilton Villas on Ballyholme Bay and the family were accomplished sailors. For Alice and her friends there were many days spent rowing about the Bay, sometimes reading poetry aloud as they went. Alice became seasick if horseplay broke out, as it occasionally did.

Her days had the unstructured aspect of the wealthier young people of the 1890's. She had no responsibilities but those she chose to accept. She met friends, went for walks, got caught in the rain, went shopping and gossiped. On a typical Sunday evening in summer a group would perhaps go 'mushrooming' in the fields around then come home and cook the mushrooms over the fire while singing songs, thought reading or playing whist. They reminisced about school, arranged more outings until it was time for bed.

A travelling fair came every summer and set up at a point on the east side of Ballyholme Bay. One of its chief attractions was a switchback ride. This entertained Alice and her friends for hours at a time.

There was also a rifle range. Alice's brother Willy, who was about twenty at this time, was a crack shot. He was in fact so successful that he was in danger of putting the fairground manager out of business. Eventually, Willy was banned from the range. His aptitudes were later used to great effect when he joined the British Army and fought in the Boer War.

This annual entertainment gave its name to Alice's "Switchback Band", which rejoiced in combs, knives and glasses as instruments. The gang of friends seems to have taken this band quite seriously for they met for frequent rehearsals.

The respectable young men of Bangor were shared out, fought over, huffed at, analysed for looks, voice and presentability in general. Politics were discussed in an opinionated way. Indeed, discussion was one of Alice's favourite pastimes. She loved to wade into the middle of it, and the more controversial the better, as, for example, this diary entry:

On the way to Belfast this morning [by train] I abused Belfast to the horror of a Presbyterian minister.

There is no evidence that she either sought or received a marriage proposal at this time. She was in her mid twenties and it would have been a natural course for her life to take.

She may have been too lively and opinionated for some of the young men who knew her. As a spirited companion she was popular, but they may not have wished to commit themselves for life to a woman who held her own views so strongly.

Her nationalist tendencies would also have made many of her Protestant friends wary of marriage to her. Later, when her circle of friends widened across the religious spectrum, she herself would not have been happy in a mixed marriage. This view comes across in her poem 'The Heretic' where even love is not strong enough to overcome the woman's objections to what the Catholic Church would ask of her:

> Ah then, farewell, though my heart should break,
> Faith I can feign not, even for love's sake.
> I plead not to Virgin nor Saint nor Martyr,
> And the soul of a child I shall never barter.

Whenever she could she went to church — Methodist or Church of Ireland — on a Sunday, sometimes twice, and was quite unfamiliar with Catholic ritual. In her writings she had to be careful. In December 1901 she was checked by A Coleman, O.P., of St. Malachy's Priory, Dundalk, who wrote to her:

I think you ought to let me see your story before sending it away, for I think you are not well up in Catholic terminology. We never speak of the Mass as a celebration, though we do speak of celebrating Mass.

It is a measure of her emotional breadth that, despite her lifelong spinsterhood, she had the insight to write of love with such feeling as she does, for example, in 'Cuisle mo Croidhe' (1904):

> Cuisle mo Croidhe, if in grief thou art,
> My soul of thy grief would share a part,
> Yes, I who adore thee would bear all pain for thee,
> Would suffer each pang of thy aching heart
> Oh love of my soul, if in grief thou art.

These and other lines make it hard to imagine that romantic love was outside her own personal experience.

It is perhaps surprising for a woman with strong and fearless views that nowhere in her diary of these bustling days does she refer to the aims and trials of the suffragette movement. She follows the politics of Ireland and its attempts to divorce itself from Britain, and comments with interest and intelligence. Apart from these occasional references her main concerns were pastimes such as gathering leaves for table decorations and rehearsing with friends a performance of the play *Bluebeard*.

Towards the end of 1891 her political persona was roughly and tragically reawakened.

On the 6th October Bangor was shrouded in heavy lowering cloud. With hindsight she described that day and night with superstitious awe:

About 5.30, just as we were dressed to start for town, a great bank of cloud swept up from the foot of the Lough, travelling low and hanging in threatening fringes right overhead; before and behind the sky was bright ... When we came along the sea from town suddenly the lightning began to blaze and run backwards and forwards across the mouth of the Lough just behind the cloud ... We sat by the fire looking out now and then at the stars and sky till after 11.00.

The next day her sister Charlotte went into the town and returned with terrible news.

Parnell was dead.

He had died suddenly at Brighton the night before.

Politically, the news was received in predictably varying ways, but the universal sentiment was shock. Alice, surrounded by her large and multifarious family found it hard to share what she felt. Her grief held a great measure of despair about Ireland's future. The Home Rule cause was, she said, "leaning on the arm of the great Liberal Party". It seemed to Alice that with Parnell also died the last hope of Irish independence. That another man of Parnell's calibre could emerge to take his place seemed unlikely indeed.

Through days of mourning, Alice carried on with her family involvements. She attended a concert in Belfast with friends on the 9th October. She felt deeply the inappropriateness of this but had a heightened sense of — as she put it — "being in the enemy's camp". In the first hints of the money problems which were to dog her later, she could not afford a ticket to Dublin to meet with people of a like mind to herself.

Her castigation of the Catholic Church for its treatment of Parnell gained renewed power. In her poem 'At Maynooth' she scathingly contrasts how the Church treated Edward VII — who as Prince of Wales had a reputation to put Parnell's in the shade — with how it treated the Irish leader.

While Alice was quite nondiscriminating in her friendships and while her many Roman Catholic friends were very good to her, she nevertheless took some harsh swipes at the hierachy.

A friend gave her a flower which had lain on Parnell's grave. It was preserved with great care.

Parnell's death was the first in a series of events which came together to dissolve an idle and carefree existence into a mood of melancholic discontent.

The next upset was more personal. In December there arrived in Belfast a young lady called Nellie Stuart. It is probable that she was the guest of friends of the Milligan's who lived near them in Belfast. Certainly she stayed with the Milligans in Bangor.

Seaton resisted the charms of Edith White but he fell passionately in love with Nell. She was popular with his brothers and sisters and even Alice liked her very much. She was remarkable for her very sweet voice and sang at the social gatherings which formed such a part of their existence. Alice was to say later that no voice in the world had ever touched her as Nell's had done. She also gained the sincere friendship of Marjorie Arthur, a fact which caused Alice some pain later.

Nellie Stuart was an only child and appears to have been rather spoilt and childish in character. This only became evident as the months went on and by then love had blinded Seaton. It seems that she had even accepted a ring from him and Alice fully expected to acquire a sister-in-law.

The sequence of events is tangled but by April 1892 it was discovered that Seaton's ring was merely one of two which Nellie had. She may indeed have collected as many as three. In England there were possibly two other young men who were under the impression that they were engaged to her.

The whole family was terribly upset and furious letters passed between Mama Milligan and Nellie's mother. It was a time of rows and tears with Seaton prostrate with grief. Such was the strain on the family that Mrs. Milligan became ill for a time.

Alice was caught in the turbulent seas around her and when later that year Seaton took his broken heart away to a post in Ceylon, he left his most devoted sister bereft. She was struggling with yet another sorrow which had meanwhile overtaken her.

Early in 1892 she was staying with friends in Cavan when she woke up during the night convinced that she could hear Marjorie Arthur calling her. Shortly afterwards she learned that Marjorie had died that night, the 5th February. Her illness was unheralded and short. In her poem 'A Nocturne', Alice refers to "the fevered night of pain before my death" (i.e. Marjorie's). This would suggest perhaps peritonitis.

Alice entrusted nothing of her feelings of bereavement to her diary. She did, however, speak in her poetry. Before this, her poems had been fairly conventional and self-conscious. Now, she had raw marrow deep feeling on which to draw and she produced some of the best poetry she ever wrote. It is non-political and non-legendary and very moving. Apart from 'A Nocturne', other poems in memory of Marjorie Arthur are 'March Violets', 'Lyrics in Memory of a Sea Lover', 'The White Wave Following', 'A Message' and 'If This Could Be'.

As these lyrics show, Alice and Marjorie had shared a rare friendship and Alice never again had a companion who came so close to her. On her bedroom wall she created what was almost a shrine to Marjorie's memory. Around her friend's photograph she

Alice's drawing of her bedroom wall where she placed
Marjorie Arthur's photograph.

arranged violets, daisies and moss. When she was
feeling depressed she would retire to her room and
give way to tears. Many times, looking at Marjorie's
picture, she would long to have access again to her
gentle wisdom.,

The circle was narrowing. Sisters Evelyn and Kathleen had left to study music in Hanover for two
years. On her birthday, St. Patrick's Day 1892, Charlotte married Charles Fox, a London solicitor. (Kathleen later married Charles' brother Robert).

Unfortunately the wedding occurred in the midst
of tensions over Nell and Seaton. For Alice it was
also uncomfortably close to the death of Marjorie.

Nevertheless it was a grand society occasion. It
took place from Royal Terrace and the bride was

dressed in green velvet. Alice had much to do arranging the flowers. There was all the usual fuss over where to sleep all the guests, and shifting of furniture to accommodate dancing and socialising. After the couple had departed there were still several more days of visiting and receiving visitors.

A few months later it was all repeated when Edith married another solicitor, George Wheeler, on 30th June.

Alice's spirits revived somewhat on her 26th birthday in September. That day she wrote a poem on the plundering of Aileach, and the completion of a poem to her satisfaction gave her an unparalleled sense of achievement. She also gives an interesting insight into her reaction to the poetry of others. She described her feelings after reading a poem by Thomas Davis:

I experienced that sudden thrill — of pain almost — creeping sensation all over — rush of tears then a chill. Walt Whitman's 'Old Ireland' and 'The West's Awake' thrilled me in the same way. Strange that one should be so physically affected by a poem.

The next day brought her a marvellous sense of well-being:

I never in my life felt in such splendid health, vigour and spirits as today.

The high point was only temporary. In October Seaton sailed for Ceylon and of the first four surviving, and emotionally closest, children of the family, only she was left. On Hallowe'en night she was greatly disturbed by inexplicable dreams in one of which Marjorie Arthur appeared, full of life and companionship.

Alice hit an abyss of depression. On one of the most emotive pages of her diary she graphically illustrates her mood. Under a sketch of a lonely stretch of shore, with her family members isolated along it, she has underlined "I feel afraid". Below this she wrote "Cha, Seaton, Edie gone — next I — but where to?"

After a traumatic twelve months there remained to her a nettle of aimlessness which she knew she had to grasp. It may be that this time of dejection acted as a catalyst, bringing into vigorous life a potential which had lain dormant and waiting for a number of years. Alice had the courage to realise that she alone held the key to her own future.

With a single minded grit entirely typical of her,

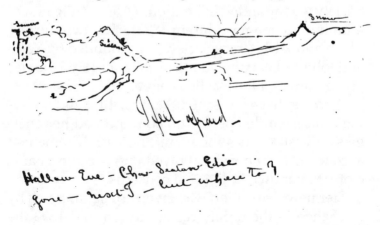

Alice's graphic expression of loneliness

she made a conscious and deliberate decision to read, write and study. After an unsuccessful attempt to return to McKillip's school in Derry, she resolved to make her own serious impression on life. She knew she could write. She had a rare knowledge of the history and legends of Ireland. She was an informed and unrepentant convert to the Irish separatist cause. Her talents and her interests came together and received the spark of opportunity and motivation which ignited a life's work.

She completed a novel, *A Royal Democrat*, and before the end of the year she had started *The Daughter of Donagh*. This was originally conceived as a novel, although it appeared eventually as a play, serialized in *United Ireland*, December 1903.

Nationally, the literary arena was at an optimum point of readiness to receive Alice and others like her, who had much to weave into the fabric of the new Gaelic movement. In 1891 The Irish Literary Society was founded in London. (Alice Milligan was admitted to membership in 1893). The twin forum, The National Literary Society, was founded by Yeats and John O'Leary in Dublin in 1892. In 1893 Douglas Hyde founded the Gaelic League.

Alice set herself a schedule of writing and studying and from this period on concentrated her energies on Irish politics and literature. Family remained a concern, but now she allowed it to become a backcloth to her own individual concerns.

Her new dedication was given crucial impetus by a change in the family residence. In mid 1893 the family moved to a new home on the Cave Hill. It was a fateful move for on the Cave Hill and Antrim Road there lived a collection of active, Irish minded people. Among them was the veteran Fenian Robert Johnston and his daughter Anna, the poetess who wrote under the name of Ethna Carbery. Young Bulmer Hobson, on whom Alice was to have some political influence, was also a neighbour.

Hobson was of Quaker stock and attended Friends School in Lisburn, Co Antrim. He became active in encouraging Ulster Protestants to join the nationalist cause and later became a vice-president of Sinn Fein and a member of the Supreme Council of the IRB.

Most notable of all was the inimitable Francis Joseph Biggar, that great patron of all things Irish, whose house, 'Ardrigh', was a major centre for Gaelic cultural enthusiasts.

At Ardrigh, Alice met and debated with those whose names became synonymous with this turbulent period. Not least of Biggar's visitors was Roger Casement.

Another of the friends she made in this significant year was William Butler Yeats. She had glimpsed him from a distance when she visited Dublin in January 1893. This was a private visit to see old friends and to read some more at the National Library and the Royal Irish Academy. She had shown some of her poetry in manuscript form to friends in Belfast and now she discovered that some acquaintances in Dublin had seen it and were very impressed. Thus her reputation as a poetess began.

One day, as she was reading in the library of the Royal Irish Academy, Yeats came in. She watched his every move, fascinated, until he departed. Some time later she went over to the National Library and was thrilled to find him there.

There he was [she wrote] writhing in the throes of composition — his long black mane floating over his eyes.

It was on this occasion also that she was introduced to George Russell (A.E.) She was taken by a friend to a meeting of the Theosophists where, she said, "mystic pictures were interpreted by a gentle stranger, Bro. Russel" (sic).

Back in Belfast she gave a lecture at the Belfast Museum on historic Ulster. This was possibly her first major speaking engagement and she was very nervous. The audience seemed unresponsive and she berated herself afterwards for talking far too long. She had hoped that this lecture might bring her one or two students whom she could teach privately, but ominously no-one approached her with such a proposal.

She continued to write poetry and to contribute to national periodicals. About this time she took a pseudonym, 'Iris Olkyrn'. Many of her works appeared over this or were simply signed 'I.O.' It is unclear why she chose to use a pseudonym. Her identity was well known and she did not hold her views in secret. 'Iris' may have been chosen because she loved flowers. 'Olkyrn' is a somewhat clumsy rendition of a family surname.

The first, and finest, of Alice's heroic poems was written this year. She got the idea for 'The Return of Lugh Lamh-Fada' when reading in the National Library in Dublin and started it on the train home. It appeared in *United Ireland* on 12th May 1893, to her great delight. The rhythm of the poem reflects the majestic subject matter and is sustained effortlessly. Writing of the Irish Civil War, the historian of the Irish troubles, P.S. O'Hegarty commented in *The Irish Statesman* in 1926:

Nobody with any acquaintance with modern Irish literature will forget Miss Alice Milligan's fine poem, 'The Return of Lugh Lamh-Fada'. [This poem] comes nearer than anything I know, than any words I can pen, to rendering how Michael Collins came to Ireland in the post 1916 years and what he meant to her ... He stands out in the red years a veritable Lugh, outstanding, gigantic, efficient.

In November Alice went with her mother to hear W.B. Yeats lecturing on Irish Fairy Lore to the Belfast Naturalists Field Club. He seemed to her to be rather nervous, but pleasingly lacking in conceit. He was introduced to her and, taking a taking a seat beside her, commented: "I hear great praise of you up in Dublin".

In a letter to Francis Joseph Biggar of 'Ardrigh' concerning his travel arrangements to Belfast for this lecture, Yeats had written:

Many thanks for your kind offer to 'dedicate' Wednesday [the day after the lecture] to my whims. I shall be indeed glad to see something of your North Country, or North Country people.

It was that very Wednesday afternoon that he

decided to visit Alice and knocked on the Milligan's door, following one of his 'whims'. At the moment he was announced Alice was on her hands and knees on her bedroom floor searching for a four-leaved shamrock which had gone missing.

This was the beginning of a rather wary literary friendship which ended only on Yeats' death in 1939.

She took him walking up the Cave Hill, although she reflected afterwards, when cleaning the mud off her boots, that perhaps this hadn't been such a good idea. On returning to the house they sat in the Library and had a long conversation about ghosts, dreams and the literary societies. He confessed to Alice that he did not have the ability to study Irish. The afternoon was peppered with interruptions by Alice's toddler brother Charles and by the bad relations between two cats and a pup. This scrimmage became so heated that Yeats took pity on the cats and picked them up onto his knee.

One consequence of Alice's friendship with Yeats, and a product of this meeting in particular, was that she began to write plays. Yeats explicitly advised her to try drama. One cannot help wondering if this was related to his somewhat enigmatic attitude to her poetry.

In a letter to Alice, dated 23rd September 1894, he returned some poems that she had sent to him for comment:

I return your poems, and only extreme amount of work keeps me from writing much more about them. I go to Ireland this week and shall meet you probably and criticize at length.

He did not take the opportunity to voice even the most platitudinous praise. He was however complimentary of her prose. He wrote to the editor of *United Ireland*, commenting on Alice's December 1893 letter (see next chapter):

'I. Olkyrn' wrote you a very beautiful letter... It is... a pleasure to be misunderstood when the misunderstanding helps to draw out so beautiful a letter.

Of a later letter to the same paper he wrote to Alice:

... your last letter to *United Ireland* reminds me that you are a very effective prose writer, and if ever the sacred anger descend upon you will do good work. (sic)

This frustrated Alice. She did not care for writing prose, and dearly wanted his praise for her poetry. Despite her voluminous output of articles, speeches, plays and novels, she saw herself always as a poet.

Despite this, Yeats' enthusiasm on the occasion of his visit induced her to re-work her novel *The Daughter of Donagh*, into a play and this is how it appeared years later, serialised in *The United Irishman* in 1903.

During the next years Alice visited Dublin as often as she could. She attended both the Theosophists and the National Literary Society where Yeats himself welcomed and introduced her. She was wholly assimilated into the literary circle and on one occasion she addressed a full meeting of the National Literary Society with a lecture on one of her favourite subjects: "Historic Tir Owen".

5

The Thick of the Fight

Yeats' visit to her was a measure of Alice's growing reputation. She was now launched on a campaign of activity which was to last into the next
century. The ethos of the Irish national literary
movement captured her imagination and her heart
and she became a tireless worker and exponent of
the creed.

Only a short month after meeting Yeats in Belfast
she encapsulated her own version of the wider philosophy by criticizing him in a letter printed on the
front page of *United Ireland* on the 16th December
1893. From some comments Yeats had made Alice
thought (wrongly) that he was opting out of politics.
She replied in words much quoted afterwards:

Irish literature cannot be developed in any hedged-in
peaceful place, whilst a conflict is raging around. It must
be in the thick of the fight, and if brought apart from it
and commanded to declare spiritual gospels to an await-
ing world, the silence will come at last....

This letter is signed with her pseudonym, Iris
Olkyrn.
One of her closest Dublin friends was John
O'Mahoney, a Cork man who was now a journalist
with the *Irish Weekly Independent*. These two may
have had a mild flirtation. They certainly spent
much time together when Alice was in Dublin, and

corresponded when she was not.

In September 1893 he wrote to her asking that she write an Ode for the anniversary of Parnell's death. Her writing, he said, would be preferred to any other.

A week later, Alice records that there came "a timid demand from Editor, *United Ireland*, for a poem — I sent him 'Sorley Buidhe'— also 'In Praise of Nial'".

O'Mahoney also encouraged her to send a wreath to be placed on Parnell's grave on his anniversary. She made one lovingly with her own hands — a chaplet of red and white dahlias — and sent it by train to Dublin. O'Mahoney collected and placed it for her.

"A chaplet of red and white dahlias." Alice's own sketch.

Throughout her life, at times of tension and excitement, she dreamed very vividly. She regarded these dreams with great seriousness and puzzled over them at length. If they referred to someone else she would write to that person and tell them of it. The whole family engaged in this and a frequent breakfast occupation of the Milligans was to relate the dreams of the night before.

At this time, when her verses were being published, when her own political and literary philosophy had crystallized into a passionate public crusade, and when the tragedy of Parnell was being replayed at his anniversary, she was again much troubled by dreams.

She dreamed very vividly of Parnell and in one disturbing sequence she stooped to pick up some ivy leaves. She put them to her lips to kiss them but they stung and pierced her fiercely like nettles and thistles. Ivy was Parnell's symbol. The anniversary of his death was called 'Ivy Day'.

In public Alice was vociferous and confident — over-assertive and opinionated for some tastes. At night, her thoughts and dreams reveal a personality perhaps a little frightened of the steps she was taking, the people who were now noticing and judging her. Two nights before Yeats visited her she had lain awake in tears, worrying about a nagging pain in her shoulder. During a fitful sleep she dreamed that her heart was being eaten out.

Subconsciously, she knew that to proceed down the path which she had deliberately sought and chosen, i.e. immersion in the new Irish national and literary movement, would be exhausting, demanding an uncompromising dedication. Given her personality, this was the only way she could serve. In 1893, it was still not too late to retreat, to conform quietly, to settle back into her secure family.

It was not in her to do that. Excitement and fervour drove her on. There were very few, if any, who knew that underneath the almost dictatorial self-confidence there lay very normal doubts and fears. Undoubtedly one of her uncertainties hinged on the methods which some Irish enthusiasts were using. When she heard of some incidents in Dublin she wrote: "A man supposed to be a spy shot dead. I feel frightened".

This assertion of feeling frightened occurs more than once in her diary. Observers of her purely public persona would never have guessed that she could feel this emotion.

Her sister Charlotte had settled with her husband Charles Fox in London and this gave Alice a base there, where she attended the Irish Literary Society and was formally accepted into membership.

As early as 1894 she was acknowledged in print along with the great names of the Literary Revival.

That year, W.P. Ryan published one of the earliest commentaries on the movement, entitled *The Irish Literary Revival: its history, pioneers and possibilities.* He wrote:

A Nation that numbers amongst its younger school such writers as W.B. Yeats, William O'Brien, Miss Barlow, Standish O'Grady, T.W. Rolleston, Edmund Downey, Frank Matthew, Francis Fahy, Dr. Hyde, Katherine Tynan, Miss Sigerson, Miss Milligan and Lionel Johnston stands in no need of ministering spirits.

Earlier in the book he writes of Alice specifically:

Miss Alice Milligan, of Belfast, is known as the authoress of many songs, of a novel *A Royal Democrat*, and as part authoress of *Glimpses of Erin*. Perhaps her best efforts are to be found in the Irish poems (somewhat unequal, however) which within the last year or so have been contributed over a nom-de-plume to the Irish press. Some of these are fine work and give hope of finer.

Ryan's analysis is interesting because he pinpoints exactly two weaknesses of the Literary Revival which the movement — and Alice Milligan most particularly — later rectified. Ryan wrote:

A weakness at present is that there is little cohesion amongst its different bodies. They have hardly a common programme; they have not a common organ ... Till they have a common system, with a spirit of real brotherhood pervading them all some of the strength of this movement will be wasted...

And he states very concisely a point which he makes more than once:

... For many of them, able as they are, there is one thing needful before they can be forces as well as units. It is a missionary spirit.

The concept of a missionary spirit is one which matches Alice's own life and work from this point on. Had she chosen the life of a full time religious, she would have brought to it an identical dedication. In a sense, Ireland became her religion. Ireland's cause was high and holy. Ireland must be served regardless of personal cost. In later years, looking back on a long life she said that Ireland and its struggle for nationhood was "the cause for which I live".

Working for Ireland was like working for salvation. She finishes her autobiographical 'Ode for the Sixth of October' with the lines:

... though thou art fallen from thy royal station
Ere the end of the ages come the world shall see
In the rising dawn of thy long afflicted nation
O Ireland dear, thy redemption come to thee.

As followers of Christ had become martyrs for their beliefs, so had the disciples of Ireland suffered and died through persecution down the centuries. This was a recurring theme in Alice's writings. In a long article, 'The North is Up!', published in the *Weekly Independent* at Christmas 1895, Alice gives an account of the '98 Rising and shows great detailed knowledge. When she relates how Henry Joy McCracken's sister Mary had wished to stay beside him when he was hanged, Alice asked:

Does it not remind one of the group of women who kept their station two thousand years ago at the foot of the Cross?

This sense of being a missionary in a sacred cause was of course shared by others. Later, notably, Patrick Pearse mingled patriotism with a religious fervour in his speeches and poetry. Alice was bound by a sense of common purpose to other fellow workers. In one of the earliest issues of *The Northern Patriot* she wrote that the paper will be:

...the meeting ground of many who differ in opinion as to the methods by which Ireland may best be served, but who have in the end one absorbing life purpose, one final goal, one common foe.

This almost spiritual devotion is evident also in the complete lack of self-interest displayed in her attitude to her work. Her poems and little plays are scattered throughout the nationalist press, in a random personal crusade for the Irish cause. She did not collect her work herself. That was left to others, particularly F. J. Biggar who so faithfully cut out and kept so much of the literary dispersion of that time.

Alice's purpose was entirely in tune with the more precise aims of the literary movement and with the newly formed Gaelic League, itself a model for missionary endeavour. She continued to write poetry as a release for her own personal emotion but now her dominating aim was political. She turned her talents to a celebration of Ireland's past, her heroes and legends. The crucial point of these poems is to reinforce Ireland's nationhood and to pull into the present years all the strength, vigour, and heroism of the past. Typical of this is 'Tara Hill is of Kings Forsaken'. The poem is a lament for the passing of Ireland's great warriors:

> .... the green sods cover
> The dust of the mighty we live to mourn.

However, the poem ascends in hope to finish with a confident rallying cry:

> No need is there to call upon Owen,
> To wish that the crown were on Brian's brow
> To long for Cormac in Tara although in Tara all is
>   desolate now;
> For the men of God's sending for Ireland's defend-

ing
Are the men he has given unto Ireland now.
(1894)

In her nostalgic assertion that Ireland's independence as a nation was the cause for which she lived, and in *The Northern Patriot*'s aim of uniting those who have "one absorbing life purpose" i.e. Ireland's independence, she effectively assigns all other contemporary concerns to the limbo of irrelevance.

Thus for her the women's suffrage movement is not an issue which distracts. As an activist in the Irish cause she is much too busy to pause over the gender issue. In fact the heroes of her political poetry follow the male stereotype. Her language is not inclusive. As in 'Tara Hill', Ireland needs marching men, brave warriors. As a child she had longed to be a boy ('When I was a Little Girl') because it was the male who was the fighter, the war machine.

Now she found that she too, could play a part, could influence events, could assail hearts and minds. This realization freed her to be an effective person and not merely an effective woman.

Commitments mushroomed around her. She took on a weekly column for the Dublin-based *Weekly Independent*, perhaps drawn in by her friendship with John O'Mahoney who continued to meet her in Dublin. He remained a friend even though she was occasionally temperamental in his company, and at least once left him standing in the rain while she became absorbed with reading in the National Library, having forgotten all about him. She was nearly locked in.

"Miss Alice Milligan of Belfast"

This column was entitled 'Notes from the North' and in it Alice is characteristically open and forthright in her views. Despite her love for the whole of the country, Alice's patch was always the North. She was proud of Ulster and much of her work involved raising the Northern voice in the Irish cause and challenging her fellows to have pride in their Irish heritage. She was glad therefore to have the opportunity to insert 'Notes from the North' into a Dublin paper.

The Irish Women's Association was set up and Alice became president of the Belfast branch in 1895. She gave an inaugural address on the 2nd November, in the Unitarian Schoolroom, Rosemary Street, Belfast. It was the first of many lectures to this Association.

This year also the Gaelic League set up a Belfast branch and Alice was at the inaugural meeting.

In April the *Weekly Independent* published one of her simplest and most effective political poems, 'Bonnie Charlie'. It scans to the tune of the popular Jacobite song but the 'Charlie' referred to is Parnell. Her fury over the treatment of Parnell — by the Irish as much as by the English — showed itself again and again through the years like a recurring fever.

W.P. Ryan, in his book on the Literary Revival, had pointed to a lack of cohesion amongst the propagandists. Politically, there was a melancholy, a low point of limbo after the death of Parnell. The guiding star had vanished. Ireland was adrift, awash with good intentions but rudderless.

Alice's organisational skills were straining to tackle the problem. Through the setting up of the Henry Joy McCracken Literary Society in Belfast in 1895 she launched what was arguably the greatest project of her life - the joint editorship of an Irish Literary newspaper.

The Henry Joy McCracken Literary Society was founded on the 9th February. Alice and others felt that there was a need for a national literary educational society because, they felt, the national education system was a mockery. Any Irish child who was subject to the ordinary course of education ended without any knowledge of the history of his or her own country.

This was one of the main motivations of Alice's work. From personal experience she knew that there was a great gap in people's knowledge of the heritage of their own country. She had after all been a teacher and many of her injunctions smack of the schoolmistress addressing well meaning but regrettably ignorant pupils.

She was one of the most vigorous members of the Henry Joy McCracken Society which met on alternate Sunday evenings. She even persuaded her sister Kathleen to sing some Irish songs to the company. On May 3rd Alice addressed the Society on the career of Hugh Roe O'Donnell. Her lecturing technique had improved enormously since her first attempt two years previously.

In August 1895 she was elected Vice-President of the Society and gave the inaugural address for the winter season. Her subject was Henry Joy himself and she spoke for an hour. *United Ireland* reported her lecture with high praise, saying that "it was one of the most able lectures ever delivered before a National body". She was received with cheers and raised great enthusiasm in her audience.

Appreciation such as this gave her encouragement and re-enforced her conviction that this was the right sphere for her undoubted talents.

The Henry Joy McCracken Society was such a success that the committee resolved to set up a library and reading room, and to publish a paper. The paper was appropriately entitled *The Northern Patriot* and the first issue appeared on the 15th October 1895, price two pence. Alice Milligan and her friend Anna Johnston (Ethna Carbery) were appointed joint editors. They took as the paper's motto "How is old Ireland and how does she stand?" from the song 'The Wearing of the Green'.

The tone of the paper is proud and, to modern ears, aggressively instructive. The editorial in the first issue stated:

We purpose at every opportunity to enlist the services of good Nationalists from several parts of the country to deliver sound and instructive addresses to our members. By this means the North will be put in touch with the other provinces, and a bond of love and union will cement all in pushing forward the good old cause that has braved unceasing persecution for seven centuries.

One of the controversial issues of the period concerned the imprisonment in England of Irishmen who had carried out a dynamiting campaign. An organisation was set up to agitate for their release. This organisation was called Amnesty and one of its chief agitators was Maud Gonne.

On the 13th November 1895, Maud Gonne, whom Alice had met before, visited the office of *The Northern Patriot* and talked at length with Anna and Alice. She was impressed with the paper and its possibilities, and promised to donate books to their library. She had an ulterior motive. She wished to enlist the services of the editors in the Amnesty cause.

Anna and Alice asked Maud Gonne to give them an article on Amnesty which they undertook to print. Miss Gonne complied, and her article entitled 'Those who are Suffering for Ireland', appeared in the paper's second issue.

Alice's attitude to issues like this bears examination. Undoubtedly she attended Amnesty meetings. Anna Johnston's father Robert was President of the Belfast Amnesty Association. The paper faithfully reported the proceedings of Amnesty Associations all over Britain.

But Alice was the product of a wealthy business family; she disliked noisy crowds; she professed fear when she heard of a violent incident. Yet she glorified in prose and verse the past struggles of Ireland and Ireland's ancient heroes. Those who in the past had "struck a blow at the tyrant" gained her starry eyed adulation. As an editor one of her main sources of copy came from the anniversaries of the martyrs, their births, their deaths, their trials, their last words.

The December 1895 issue emblazons the words "The Boys who are true to Erin, Oh!" and states:

We purpose monthly publishing an account of a battle in which Irishmen in the past showed conspicuous heroism.

Another regular item was "The Month's Martyrs". These undeniable facts must be set alongside the powerful editorial comments made in October 1896. They are worth quoting at length. The editorial is entitled 'Guard Ireland's Honour' and is preceded by the pointed quotation:

For freedom comes from God's right hand,
And needs a Godly train;

And righteous men shall make our land
A nation once again.

... We believe for our part that the feeling of the country on the subject [of dynamite methods] is entirely abhorrent, and that it is everywhere recognised that those who would stoop to suggest, or organise, or carry out anything of the sort, degrade the name and fame of their country, and in the eyes of the whole world render her less worthy of Nationhood. Ireland's cause is high and holy: When Irishmen cease to regard it as so, the faith which has sustained the strife of ages will perish and she will sink into hopeless bondage.

We are fond of finishing off announcement of our National gatherings with the martyrs' prayer of "God Save Ireland", and we must see to it that the devil is not enlisted as chief auxiliary to realize that salvation. Stern and terrible deeds are often done and may justly be done in such a strife as ours; but this method of bomb throwing and blowing up buildings, without aim or reason other than mere desire for vengeance is imbecile and wrong.

These words must be read carefully. They are not, as might first appear, advocating total non-violence. What Alice clearly does not condone are the tactics of random terror. This was "enlisting the devil" and reducing Ireland to the gutter.

In the wider political thinking of the period, the new doctrine of Communism had led some people to the further conclusion that an ideal world would have no laws and acknowledge no authority - in a word that Alice uses just before the piece quoted: Anarchism.

This is what Alice so firmly castigates. She had a high romantic view of Ireland's honour and dignity. Noble nations have disciplined armies, they do not tolerate freelance action by those who break ranks and fire before the word is given. So, while everyone might understand their motives, no quarter can be given to those who may lose the war before the true army has a chance to fight.

Nevertheless, at this time in her life — aged thirty — she does not renounce the concept of a just war if it should be necessary. She idealized organization, strategy, discipline and self-denying obedience to orders. Her romantic visions were of marching soldiers and green flags flying.

Twenty years later she was to taste the difference between romance and reality.

Anna and Alice's editorship of *The Northern Patriot* survived for only three issues. There was a split on policy with the parent Society. What exactly caused this split is hard to pinpoint. Anna and Alice either resigned or were sacked. The latter is more probable. The January 1896 issue appeared with the following front page "Notice To Readers" :

Our readers will observe that we have made a change in the Editorship of THE NORTHERN PATRIOT. We were reluctantly compelled to take this step in order to keep our journal from becoming the weapon of any political party in Irish political life ... THE NORTHERN PATRIOT is a journal of the people; we shall never allow it to become an organ of faction.

Either the Amnesty issue was behind this or perhaps Alice's pro-Parnellite sympathies were a little too strong. The paper's original aim was to steer a neutral course through the various Irish factions which were jostling each other in these awkward years. Alice was an unashamed and vociferous Parnellite with total disdain for other more compromising stances. (This is illustrated, for example, by her pair of sonnets 'Then and Now: a contrast', published in *United Ireland*, September 1893).

Whatever the cause of the disagreement, Anna and Alice did not take time to draw breath. When the new editor of *The Northern Patriot* brought out issue number four in January 1896, he found he was sharing the news stands with a new paper: *The Shan Van Vocht*. The editor was Miss Alice Milligan and the secretary was Miss Anna Johnston.

The indefatigable pair kept the same printer, found a new office at Anna's father's timber yard, and carried on. The rival publications appeared simultaneously for nearly two years but it was an unequal battle. *The Northern Patriot* reduced its price to one penny but without effect. The last issue appeared on 15th November 1897. *The Shan Van Vocht* remained confidently at two pence.

The title is an ancient name for Ireland, meaning 'the poor old woman'. The stirring motto chosen was from another song:

> Yes, Ireland shall be free,
> From the centre to the sea
> And hurrah liberty
> Says the Shan Van Vocht.

This paper came to have a wide circulation. An agent was appointed in New York to organise distribution in America. Rumour had it that issues of the 'Shan', as it was fondly known, were read surreptitiously beneath desks in Dublin Castle.

Alice was now working at full stretch and she was supremely happy. Her family's reactions to her preoccupations were mixed but usually remarkably tolerant. One incident did hurt her very much. Her sister Edith, married to solicitor George Wheeler and of Unionist persuasion, invited her parents and family for an evening get together. Alice was pointedly left out of the invitation. It was a gratuitous snub which was keenly felt. Political divergence did not give Alice an indifference to her family.

The Shan Van Vocht was greatly admired and the editor became even more well known than before. Seumas McManus, the Donegal writer and storyteller (who later married Anna Johnston) commented "... these brave girls revived Irish nationalism when it was perishing". In a forward to a later volume of poetry, Seumas McManus' tribute is even more flamboyant:

When, after the débacle of the nineties the Irish cause was at lowest ebb, the morale of even brave men broken, and boldest fighters in retreat, two Belfast girls - poets - Alice Milligan who had smashed off her shackles of alienism whereunto she was born, and Ethna Carbery ... stepped in the gap and in noble numbers sounded an electrifying rallying call.

Alice might have taken him up on his "shackles of

alienism" comment. She never laboured the fact of her Protestantism — it was irrelevant to her politics, and personally she never renounced her religious descent. If she thought about it at all it was with a sense of annoyance that Catholic Irishmen should try to imply that she was less Irish than they; that absence of a Rosary should mean absence of patriotism. It was an attitude that many Protestant nationalists found irritating.

Alice took a few lines in *The Shan Van Vocht* to insert a quotation from Thomas Davis:

Reader, if you be an Irish Catholic, and that you confound the Protestant religion with tyranny, learn from Grattan that it is possible to be a Protestant and have a heart for Ireland and its people. Think that the brightest age of Ireland was when Grattan, a steady Protestant, raised it to proud eminence and also that in the hour of his triumph he did not forget the state of your oppressed fathers, but laboured through his virtuous life that both you and your children should enjoy unshackled liberty of conscience.

Alice's newspaper was an early vehicle for the views of an almost unheard of Socialist called James Connolly. Two of his articles which Alice printed were titled 'Can Irish Republicans be Politicians?' and 'Nationalism and Socialism'. He argued that some of the literary societies and committees which had sprung up were in danger of being entrenched in the past, of idealizing past glory to the extent that they were impotent to help in Ireland's present and future. It was a point which stung Alice.

Her younger brother Ernest had to visit Dublin for an examination and Alice asked him to visit Connolly and report back to her. Ernest (a member of the Gaelic League) was very impressed by what he found, to the extent that he joined Connolly's Irish Socialist Republican Party, formed a Belfast branch and helped distribute their newspaper, *Irish Worker*. The paper's sales declined and finally publication ceased. Ernest's involvement was sincere but brief. He was probably very influenced by his much older sister. The search for employment took him to England and he left the stage.

In the pages of *The Shan Van Vocht* can be heard the first faint breaths of the infant Sinn Fein movement — Arthur Griffith's non-violent Sinn Fein of the early years of the twentieth century. Alice was amongst those, such as Maud Gonne, who felt that to negotiate further with the English Parliament for Home Rule was to prostitute the honour of Ireland. Her poem, 'Westminster 1895' lucidly illustrates this:

> O Irishmen, not here, not here
> Should Freedom's boon be longer sought,
> Nor to our foe's disdainful ear,
> Demands for Nationhood be brought....
>
> ... Let none debase our country's name
> Stooping to crave her freedom here.

Alice voiced a lessening of enthusiasm for the Home Rule Bill after Parnell's death because she did not want an Englishman — Gladstone — to get the acclaim. She would rather have had it postponed until another Irish leader could get the credit.

Such was the affection in which the paper was held that Anna and Alice visited different parts of the country addressing meetings of supporters. On one such occasion they visited Maud Gonne in Dublin. In her autobiography, *A Servant of the Queen*, Miss Gonne recalls:

It had been one of our late nights in my rooms over Morrow's Library (on the corner of Nassau Street and Frederick Street), for Anna Johnston and Alice Milligan from Belfast were staying in Dublin and Anna had read us some of her poems and we were full of almost envious admiration of some numbers of *The Shan Van Vocht* the daring little paper Anna and Alice were editing. They were so different but worked so well together — Anna tall and romantic with her long face and tender dreamy eyes — Alice small aggressive and full of observant curiosity. I thought Dublin would have to look to its laurels if it were not to be outdone in literary journalism by Belfast.

Douglas Hyde, one of Alice's long standing friends and a frequent correspondent down the years, also contributed poems and articles.

Despite all the interest and articles donated, Alice herself wrote much of the copy for the paper. She churned out stories, poems, historical essays and editorials. This, together with a full speaking diary, meant that her life was completely taken over.

Her desire to educate and exhort the people led her to set up Home Reading Circles, co-ordinated by the newspaper. She laid down rules. They were to consist of six to twelve members. One member was to be appointed librarian and send to her a list of all the books the group had. She would collate all the lists and produce a complete catalogue. The Secretary of the Circle had to ensure that members actually read the books. Each member was also to undertake to buy new books for the Circle. If each of twelve members bought four books then forty eight volumes would be added to each group per annum.

Alice herself visited the groups and told them what they should be reading. Charm and transparent sincerity sweetened the exhausting enthusiasm for she was popular despite her rather didactic approach.

In 1899 Arthur Griffith and William Rooney launched a new weekly newspaper *The United Irishman* and through it began to argue the case for national self reliance and possible resistance to English rule. The monthly *Shan Van Vocht*'s work was taken over by a publication with more resources than its own. Alice was in full sympathy with Griffith and did not wish to dilute his efforts. Anna and Alice took the difficult and sad decision to close their paper. The last issue appeared on 6th March 1899, two days after the first issue of *The United Irishman*. They sent the list of their subscribers to Griffith.

Alice received a somewhat cryptic letter from a correspondent in Killybegs who said:

I'm very sorry about the suspension of the S.V.V. but under the circumstances perhaps a decent death was better than some other things that might have happened the paper.

It is tempting to think that Alice may have been relieved to relinquish the undoubted strain and pressure of the previous three and a half years. Anna was shortly to marry Seumas McManus and go to live with him in Donegal. This would have posed a difficulty for the paper for it was, since the split with the Henry Joy McCracken Literary Society, very much the product of two individuals.

It is more likely that she regretted the disappearance of a medium which so wholly occupied one of the high points of her happiest years. Just after the last issue of the *Shan Van Vocht* appeared, Alice became unwell. The nature of this illness is unknown, but was enough to cause concern to her friends. Msnr. McFadden wrote to her from Donegal on the 10th, sending his good wishes. He addresses her as 'My very dear friend'.

Perhaps this illness was caused by a psychological reaction to the loss of her newspaper and the all-consuming work which went with it. This is only speculation although certainly she received much sympathy and concern from her wide circle of friends.

In time she recovered, aware that she could not allow a tedious and depressing void to engulf her. She was an apostle, she still had work to do.

Griffith and Rooney had cause to be grateful to her. *The United Irishman* (which later became *Sinn Fein*) was launched onto ground that had been well tilled by others.

Sorrow and Success

Students of the period have given many reasons for the explosion of political, cultural and literary activity during the years following Parnell's death. Many chips of a mosaic fitted together to produce a picture of popular national awareness. One of the brightest colours in this mosaic was the occasion of the Centenary of the 1798 rebellion by the United Irishmen under Wolfe Tone.

The leaders of nationalist consciousness saw it coming and determined to make the most of it. Commemoration Committees, under a Central Executive, were set up all over the country. It was seen as an opportunity to educate and arouse the people to separatist sympathies through memorial ceremonies, meetings and lectures.

As much as two years before the Centenary itself, committees were making plans. Alice Milligan was appointed Organising Secretary for the Centenary celebrations in Ulster. As she was at this time still editing *The Shan Van Vocht* one wonders where she found enough hours in the day for her multitudinous interests.

Yeats caused one of the headaches which went with the job. He was finalising plans for the first productions of The Irish Literary Theatre and was concerned at the clash of date. He wrote to Alice asking that she postpone the Belfast '98 Celebrations until 1899, to enable him to stage his plays in Belfast in 1898. This caused a rift in the committee. Alice was indignant at the request, and the situation called for John O'Leary's diplomacy. The Celebrations were not postponed.

In 1898 Alice published, from the offices of *The Shan Van Vocht*, her topical *Life of Theobald Wolfe Tone*. She was knowledgeable on all the Irish heroes of the past, but Wolfe Tone was a particular favourite. The book brought together her considerable learning on the 1798 rebellion which had been amassed for the many lectures she had given. The eulogistic work was dedicated to Miss Kate A Maxwell of Brooklyn, New York, Tone's great-grand daughter.

Maud Gonne, John O'Leary and William Rooney were amongst the leaders of the celebrations. These, together with Anna Johnston and Alice, toured the country delivering lectures on the United Irishmen. The lectures were well attended, particularly in the country areas where many poorer people walked miles to hear them.

Alice had a great admiration for John O'Leary, the noble dignified old Fenian leader from an earlier generation. After twenty years imprisonment and exile he had returned to Ireland on condition that he took no part in political activity. Unavoidably, he occupied a position of eminence and reverence from which he influenced and guided with a gentlemanly dedication. Yeats acknowledged himself to be O'Leary's pupil "in many things".

After Commemoration Committee meetings in Dublin, he would escort Alice home, and would not leave her until she was safely at the door of her lodgings in Merrion Square.

Alice invited him to Belfast to speak at the Belfast Centenary celebrations. While in the city he stayed at the Milligan's home and was photographed there.

Some of the more Unionist family members were outraged. "Imagine having *that* man in the house!" exclaimed Edith indignantly.

One must again pay tribute to the tolerance — and indeed courage — of Alice's mother and father. Unlike her siblings, there is no indication that they subjected their fiery daughter to censure or vociferous disapproval. Around the end of the century Alice's mother began to have periods of ill health which caused the family some worry. This was a foreshadowing of family illness which was to become such an inhibiting factor in Alice's later career.

For now, despite occasional spells when duty kept her at home, her parents saw little of her. She became a veteran traveller by train and coach. No sooner had she gathered some money kindly given to pay expenses than she had passed it across the counter of yet another ticket office. The railway network was much more extensive then than is evident from the pathetic remnants of today.

She did not pause for breath between engagements. For example, on May 11th 1896 she lectured on Red Hugh O'Donnell at the Gaelic Language Congress in Donegal. On May 14th she lectured on The King's Chieftains at Tir-owen to the William Collins Branch of the National Foresters at Strabane. June 1st she was in Omagh and her subject was Hugh Roe O'Donnell. During the Centenary Celebrations in 1898 her schedule was even more punishing. On 24th January she spoke at the Dundalk Centenary Celebrations. The next day she was in Derry to speak to their Celebration meeting.

The Shan Van Vocht detailed all the Centenary meetings and carried an advertisement for a jewellery works in Belfast which was acting with good business sense by offering for sale a range of '98 commemoration jewellery - badges, brooches, cufflinks, etc.

Alice had joined the Belfast Branch of the Gaelic League as soon as it was formed. When a fervently held belief has brought people together into an organization created for the purpose of spreading this creed, then gender differentiation is an unaffordable luxury. Thus the Gaelic League recruited men and women on equal terms, glad of anyone who volunteered for their "mission field". In the Autumn, Anna Johnston, Seumas McManus and Alice went on a 'Donegal Crusade' along the route of The County Donegal Railway, visiting Killybegs, Glenties, Glencolmcille and Glenfin. They told stories, put on short plays and tableaux and worked to raise the Irish national consciousness of the ordinary people.

One of the major concerns of the Gaelic League was to encourage the spread of the Irish language and in this Alice was an enthusiast also. Since her days in Dublin she had tried to study Irish for at least some part of every day. During the summers at Bangor she would sit by the switchback poring over a little primer. For all her Irish passion she found the language very difficult. In old age she recalled it as the toughest task she had ever set herself. Others like her gave up the struggle. Maud Gonne learnt a few sentences merely to introduce her speeches. Alice's interest was genuine and persistent. Like her friend Douglas Hyde, she believed in "The Necessity of De-anglicizing Ireland" and what she asked others to do, she was determined to do herself.

Her progress was slow and never perfect. In 1896, when speaking at the Gaelic League Congress in Donegal she was one of only three speakers to use English. *The Shan Van Vocht* reported the occasion:

.... Miss Milligan used the Saxon tongue with humble apologies and promises to work hard and do better next time.

At the age of forty six, hearing some anecdotes of Roger Casement's illustrating the point that Protestant Ulster had spoken Gaelic in days past, she recalled her own childhood on her uncle's farm in Omagh, where Irish was spoken even yet. She reflected ruefully:

... yet here I am, you see, with not much Gaelic to boast of, though I was one of the first and most fervent starters.

The problem and the passion remained with her. At the age of seventy six, speaking in Omagh, she regretted that she could not express her thoughts, hopes and principles in "a sufficiently lucid style in the Irish tongue, "though she was busy learning it all the time.

She did attain some level of competence to the

point where she attempted some plays in Irish. Many of the little plays which she and Anna Johnston staged on their tours were written by Alice, e.g. *Cu Chulainn* and *Diarmaid agus Grainne*. On 3rd April 1899 she produced *Naomh Padraig ag an Teamhair* (*St. Patrick at Tara*) in St. Colm's Hall, Derry. She herself played the part of Lady in Waiting to the Queen.

The partnership between Anna Johnston and Alice was a rewarding one. Their plays and tableaux were admired widely. At Easter 1900, William Rooney invited them both to Dublin to present their productions before a Gaelic League gathering.

During a restful period in Autumn 1899, at home in the Villa 'Eastward' in Bangor, where the Milligans now — and finally — resided ("We're moving no more! "said Mama Milligan) Alice was immensely thrilled and flattered when Standish O'Grady arrived at her gate on his bicycle one sunny evening. O'Grady had heard as much of her as she had of him and wished to meet her.

They spent many evenings talking for hours about the glories of Ulster. O'Grady and Alice had a common experience in that their youthful education had contained nothing of Ireland and they were both largely self taught.

Others were approaching the issue of raising Irish national awareness in their own way. Yeats had begun his friendship with Lady Gregory of Coole Park in County Galway. These two were amongst the strongest believers in an Irish literary culture being an essential prerequisite of an Irish nation. If Ireland had a tradition of artistic merit which was singularly Irish and not — like the works of Shaw and Wilde — Anglo-Irish, then her case for being regarded as an autonomous nation would be strengthened.

Yeats and Lady Gregory founded the Irish Literary Theatre to stimulate progress towards this goal. The first production, Yeats' *Countess Cathleen*, was staged in 1899. This company was to evolve into the world famous Abbey Theatre.

Alice Milligan was quick to seize the opportunity to submit some of her own work for consideration, and had the thrill of seeing her short play *The Last Feast of Fianna* staged by the company.

The Last Feast was performed on February 19th, 1900, along with Edward Martyn's *Maeve*. It lasted only twenty minutes but W. J. Feeney, in a preface to an edition of the play observed that::

The Last Feast of the Fianna is the first completely Celtic Twilight play in setting, characters and theme... For Alice Milligan there remains the honour of being the first playwright to dramatise Celtic legend for an Irish audience.

Amongst the literary giants of the time, Alice Milligan is thus credited as an innovator.

A contemporary Daily Express critic (an Irish paper, no relation of the present English one of the same name) was impressed enough to write:

If the aim of the Irish Literary Theatre is to create national drama it is obvious that the development of Miss Milligan's method is the proper road to reach ultimate success.

Yeats wrote fulsomely and typically:

Miss Milligan's little play delighted me because it has made in a very simple way and through the vehicle of Gaelic persons, that contrast between immortal beauty and the ignominy and mortality of life which is the central theme of ancient art.

Also typically, Alice refuted this esoteric interpretation of her play:

I simply wrote it on thinking out this problem; how did Oisin endure to live in the house with Grania as stepmother after all that had happened?

The Theatre published a magazine, *Beltaine*, and Yeats asked Alice to write an article for it giving the legendary background to her play, to put it in context for those who saw it. In her comments in this article we can detect a woman much changed from the impressionable, excitable girl who had hopped up and down on a tram when she saw Parnell and who had loved to saunter round Stephen's Green and hold intellectual conversations in Trinity College.

She was now in her mid thirties and more cynical, more acerbic in her public utterances. In *Beltaine* she pointed out that the very fact of being asked to provide background for her play was an indictment of "the Dubliners and Trinity College intellectuals who neither understand nor respect the literature of ancient Ireland". An audience of Kerry peasants, she said, would have no need of background information.

She had been part of the Dublin and Trinity College intellectual set and had moved far from it. Her natural hinterland now was rural Ireland, the peasantry whom she idealised and romanticised in her verse. These were the pure in heart, the hope of the nation, and if they spoke Irish, they were even nearer to heaven's gate.

She never again had a play staged by this illustrious theatre, although she did try. In the Autumn of 1901 she sent the manuscript of her play *The Daughter of Donagh* to Lady Gregory. To her intense disappointment, the following January, Lady Gregory returned it. Yeats apparently considered that it changed scene too often to be a practical proposition.

Nevertheless, many of her little plays and tableaux were scattered throughout the press and were staged proudly at feisanna countrywide. At least one of her plays is said to have had a significant effect on Yeats. He wrote in his autobiography:

I saw William Fay's amateur company play Miss Milligan's *Red Hugh*, an historical play on the style of Walter Scott. I came away with my head on fire.

It has been said that this inspired his own famous play *Cathleen ni Houlihan*.

The full title of Alice's play was *The Escape of Red Hugh*. The role of St. Bridget was played by Sinead O'Flanagan, who later married Éamon de Valera. When de Valera escaped from Lincoln Prison in 1919, Alice wrote the poem 'Merely Players' in which she reminded Sinead of the staging of this play:

Memory holds a girlish picture of you,
Kneeling, with a Celtic cross above you,
Under the saintly Brigid's cloak of blue;
Innocent and fair to all beholders,
With your rippling hair about your shoulders,
When we staged the drama of Red Hugh.

So when came your hour of heaviest sorrow,
Words of mine your prayerful lips could borrow;
Prayer for such deliverance as he knew,
Who from Dublin on a night of snowing
Fled with his companions, onward going
Over hills and vales of Wicklow through.

In 1901 Alice lost her closest friend and partner
when Anna Johnston married Seumas McManus
and went to live with him in Revlin, Co. Donegal. It
was a beautiful place with which Alice was familiar.
Her poem 'The House of the Apple Trees, No.1'
commemorates this marriage and in it Alice looks
forward to visiting her friend in her new home:

And some day in the spring's delightful weather
I will be with you, we will see together
The hawthorn at its whitest and the whin
In hills of living gold ...

Alice's friendships were dogged by tragedy. The
next Spring which Alice had so looked forward to,
she did indeed visit Revlin, but only because Anna
had died in The House of the Apple Trees. The
second of her poems of that title hauntingly describes

this harrowing visit and the apple trees, now "gaunt and bare-branched":

> I know they will be beautiful in May,
> But - she has gone away.

Seumas McManus spent much of the rest of his long life in the U.S.A. and died in New York in 1960.

Alice's impression of her younger sister Evelyn

For the second time Alice had lost an intimate friend who had shared much of her eventful life. In 1901 William Rooney, Alice's friend and co-founder of the *United Irishman* had also died tragically early at the age of 29. Alice commemorates Rooney in verse in her poem 'At The Graveside'.

Tragedy followed tragedy. Just over a year after Anna's death, the Milligan family suffered searing bereavement when Alice's sister Evelyn drowned by walking straight out to sea at Bangor. She was twenty eight. The youngest child, Charles, who was a young teenager at the time, was on the shore and watched horrified as Evelyn disappeared. The effect on the family was traumatic. Charles never felt able to talk about it in later years.

Mrs. Milligan never fully recovered from the tragedy. Her health was already indifferent and declined further over the next years. Evelyn is buried in the family plot at Drumragh, Omagh.

By contrast, Alice's literary life was flourishing. She was one of that coterie of young poets which George Russell had gathered around him in Dublin. Russell was a supporter of female suffrage and an enthusiastic patron of aspiring writers, encouraging and admonishing them. Alice Milligan was one of whom he thought most highly. He took a personal pride in these poets and used his influence to further their careers. In a letter written in 1902, he said:

There are many poets here who write beautiful lyrics who are quite unknown out of Ireland ... I have seen many verses signed 'I.O.', 'Alice Milligan', 'Ethna Carbery', 'Oghma', 'Paul Gregan'. which I enviously wish I could claim as my own ... I think myself many of these unknown poets and poetesses write verses which no living English writer could surpass.

In 1904, Russell made a start at rectifying what he saw as neglect of talent. He brought out a slim volume of verses called *New Songs*. It cost one shilling and sixpence and included an etching of 'The Plougher' by W.B. Yeats' brother Jack. The five poems by which Alice was represented were the first of her verses to appear in book form.

George Russell, in his forward to the book, picks out Alice for particular mention, saying that it is his belief that she wrote the best patriotic poetry of Ireland in his lifetime. Yeats and Russell, who had been close collaborators, were now somewhat more distant in their dealings with one another. Russell's interest in so many young poets was partly behind the cooling. Russell suggested to Yeats that it would greatly help the sale of *New Songs* — and consequently the reputation of the poets — if Yeats were to publicly praise the volume. Yeats refused rather haughtily and penned some cutting lines to Russell entitled 'To a poet, who would have me praise certain bad poets, imitators of his and mine':

> You say, as I have often given tongue
> In praise of what another's said or sung,
> 'Twere politic to do the like by these;
> But was there ever dog that praised his fleas?

By this time Alice had discarded her pseudonym, Iris Olkyrn, and acknowledged all her work by her own name. Reflecting her increasing involvement in the crusade for the propagation of the Irish language, she began to use the Irish form of her name — Eilis ni Maeleagain.

Financially her writing brought both rewards and liabilities. In 1903 the printers Alfred Nutt of London sent her a bill of £5.12.6 for the printing of *The Last Feast of the Fianna*. She never kept accounts. Enough cash in hand for the next project or the next journey was sufficient.

In 1908 George Russell edited the first volume

dedicated to solely to Alice's verse, — *Hero Lays*. This volume of her patriotic verse, gathered from newspapers and journals, brought together her versions of legendary tales from which she drew parallels with the present struggle for Irish freedom.

Her most famous poem 'When I was a Little Girl' was included in *Hero Lays*. Its inclusion is owed to Russell's insistence, for Alice did not want it in the collection. Russell's letter to her on the subject is vivid and humorous, revealing much of Russell's personality. It was written from the offices of *The Irish Homestead*, the agricultural journal which Russell was editing:

Dear Alice Milligan,

I am not going to yield to you about that child poem. Not unless you are going to make a death or glory business out of it. I have too much respect for that little girl who chases the black-coated police to oust her out because a bigger girl is terrified because of black coated priests: Seriously I don't think that poem would install anybody not even a Unionist. The hostility to the Fenian movement is dead as the movement has become part of history and the record of a child's enthusiasm is not going to stir up any antagonism now. Please please leave it in ... It will be recited at Convent schools and taught by nuns in preference to any other poem in the book. I won't give it up to you, that's flat! Now what have you to say. Its your move. My cards are on the table. Are you going to fight? The story of your little night dressed Fenian has put fire into me and in the name of that child I confront you and defy you. Do your worst!

Yours, A.E.

As she passed into the first decade of the twentieth century, there was a dichotomy in Alice's view of life. Her tendency to morbidity and to the idolizing of the dead perhaps had its beginnings as far back as 1891 with the death of Parnell. But despite this tragedy and the deaths of three of her siblings in childhood, no other bereavement so deeply affected her as the death of Marjorie Arthur in 1892. At the age of twenty six, her extrovert, bubbly personality had been given pause and sorrow made its first deep cut.

As other bereavements followed her thoughts were pulled more and more to the dead and their influence on the living. This concept was compounded by Alice's study of the ancient Irish heroes. For her, they spoke eloquently to the present day and drove her on in her crusade for Irish freedom.

She saw the Cavehill, overlooking her Belfast home, as a monument to Russell, Tone and McCracken. In the *Weekly Independent* of Christmas 1895 she told readers that "it reminds us of the noble dead".

In another very poignant article in which she describes some days spent nursing, relieving the sisters of a young friend who was dying, she meditates on death:

I told him how all my own inspirations came, not from those who were busy in the living world, so much as from the dead. It is they above all whose wishes, when we remember them, are commands we dare not shrink from obeying, whose unfulfilled hopes we treasure tenderly ... I spoke the name of a friend who died long, long ago, and whose memory is in all the poetry that people tell me is my best.

She refers also to herself and her fellow workers as those "whose bonds are with the dead comrades in a vanquished and vanished army".

In a very real sense, her motivation was derived from an obligation to the dead, both ancient and contemporary, to carry out their wishes, to carry on the fight and be their worthy successor.

With the exception of her parents, all whom Alice loved deeply, died before their time.

In contrast to this underlying conviction, the coming of the twentieth century carried on for Alice a very happy and creative phase. As a writer she was achieving success. She had a play produced by Yeats' theatre. Two books of poetry contained her verses, one of them her own exclusively.

Despite the recurrent illness of her mother which kept Alice at home occasionally, she now demonstrated quite a flair for humorous verse. Poems such as 'Up the Falls (Springtime)' and 'To the Most Beautiful' demonstrate a sense of fun and mimicry which she did not often take time to indulge.

When an editor in Boston, U.S.A., wrote to her asking if he might include some of her verses in a compilation of Victorian Verse she refused in verse with a touch that was light and deadly. Her poem 'In Answer' finishes thus:

> We in Ireland have reckoned the reign and the
> years
> Of Victoria, in famine, rebellion and tears.
> By the chains of John Mitchel,
> By the loss of Parnell,
> (Foulest wrong since the hour

When TirChonaill's Hugh fell)
By these griefs, by these wrongs,
I refuse you my songs,
More in sorrow than anger,
                    Alice Milligan, Bangor.

She also wrote some very beautiful love poetry.
One must remember, if one is to get a proper per-
spective on the character of Alice Milligan, that the
same pen which castigates England and glorifies ancient heroes, also wrote lines such as these:

Love let me know if you should come to sit
Beside my grave to sorrow over it,
When I am dead;
Would you not pity one whose life was spent?
Would love of pity born make you repent
The words you said?
You answer so; then dearest, must I die
To earn your love, since sorrow by and by
Will not undo
The pains I suffer now? Then lest it be
As I foretell, look kindlier on me.

It is almost impossible to believe that the writer of
'Cuisle mo Croidhe' and 'Fada an La' had never
experienced the emotion they describe. If she herself did love like this, it is a secret well hidden from
posterity.

Darling Little Battery

For five years, between the cessation of the *Shan Van Vocht* in 1899 and the publication of *New Songs* in 1904, Alice did not have any overwhelming commitments other than those she chose to undertake in writing and drama. She remained a dedicated traveller and member of the literary societies. As a member of the Gaelic League she contributed as much as she could when time, talents and family pressures permitted.

In 1900, when Maud Gonne founded the revolutionary feminist women's society, 'Inghinidhe na h'Eireann' ('Daughters of Ireland') she asked Alice and Anna Johnston for their help and expertise in staging plays under the auspices of the new organisation. They gladly co-operated.

Alice filled her own timetable and was happy to a certain extent. Her father was Vice-President of the Royal Society of Antiquaries of Ireland and it was on their tour in 1901, when the Society visited the Western Hebrides, that Alice was moved to immortalize Marjorie Arthur yet again in the poem 'The White Wave Following'.

After the death of Anna Johnston in 1902 and her sister Evelyn in 1903, Alice found herself restless. Her dynamic approach to Irish affairs was not channelled into a structured sphere of operation. When in 1904, the Gaelic League advertised for Lantern Lecturers, it was an opportunity Alice could not ignore. Despite enforced spells at home when her mother was unwell, she was not what might be termed a 'domesticated' woman. She had to be on the move, teaching and exhorting to the limit of her strength.

The Gaelic League at this time was enjoying increasing success and influence. It had nearly 600 branches countrywide, still not at the maximum which it achieved before its rapid decline in the 1920's.

The aims of the League were simple. It wished to record and preserve the native folklore still surviving in the Irish speaking districts and to rescue this culture from extinction; to reverse the process and spread the Irish language through literature and music. The League campaigned to introduce the Language into schools and universities so that a sense of Irish identity, owing nothing to the supplanting English language, would spread throughout the country.

Item 8 of the Gaelic League's constitution states unequivocally:

The League shall be strictly non-political and non-sectarian.

At the time when Alice was working for the League, item 8 was a reality. Douglas Hyde had a vision that all Irishmen could be united by a common love for Ireland and its language. Perhaps inevitably, this ideal could not survive the intensity of political thinking which infiltrated it over the ensuing years through active members such as Patrick Pearse. In 1915 Hyde resigned his Presidency of the League.

In November 1904, however, Alice received her letter of appointment as a Lantern Lecturer. She was sent straight to Co. Cork at the other end of the country.

At home family matters had stabilised fairly well after the death of Evelyn. Her brother William had left for Chicago where he was to spend about ten years. Sister Charlotte founded the Irish Folk Song Society this year also, and Alice joined its publications committee. With her politically opposite sister Edith, she worked with Charlotte in composing words for some of the native music which Charlotte gathered.

After the tragedies of Anna Johnston and her sister Evelyn, and on a crest of success creatively after the publication of *New Songs*, Alice took off for Cork with an enthusiasm which touched all who came into contact with her.

The work was highly demanding but for Alice it was the breath of life. She had new direction, an organisation to work for, aims to achieve. *The Leader* in January 1905 noted her appointment and commented:

In appearance she is small and slight and one wonders how so much energy can be contained in so small a frame.

She had to compile for herself a systematic plan of work and fill in a daily itinerary which was submitted to her superiors showing how her time was spent. Inevitably, she came into contact with many people. She called on the local clergy and others of influence in the area to increase publicity and, if possible, to have any meetings she might arrange announced from the pulpit. She set up language classes and classes for music and Irish dancing.

By encouraging new members of the League, workers such as Alice were helping to build up the finances of the organisation. Its administrative expenses were entirely met by voluntary subscription and reached £6,000 per year.

Where ever she went she made an impression. She seems to have been quite without self-consciousness in her immersion in her work. It was during her time in Cork that she met the O'Donovan Rossa's and earned their affection. Mary O'Donovan Rossa's letter is worth quoting again in this context. It was written on Christmas eve 1905, from Blackrock, Co Cork:

Dear Miss Milligan,

I need not ask is your sister better. You are with her and you are a darling little electric battery - a little storehouse of vitality in whose vicinity the miasmatic vapours of sickness and melancholy are simply impossible of existence ... (We) have taken a very great liking to you ... One of those beneficent impulses may seize your headlong spirit to dive (sic) through Cork on your way to the North, and if so, Oh please let us know, that we may warm ourselves in your sunny atmosphere more speedily. I'm going to make Rossa laugh reading this letter him ....

I remain, dear Miss Milligan,
Yours sincerely,
Mary J O'Donovan Rossa.

From Cork Alice was once again sent the length of the country to County Derry, a country which she knew and loved well. By January 1906 she had completed a tour of County Antrim and had moved on to County Donegal.

Despite her work for the Gaelic League, Alice never ceased to write. She kept in contact, in person and by letter, with George Russell, who was planning her volume *Hero Lays* which appeared in 1908. Her verses continued to appear in the press and we know from the comments of others that they were not merely editorial spacefillers. Her verses were solicited and deeply appreciated.

Joseph McGarrity, writing to her many sad years later in 1934, told her:

.... I assure you that for thirty five years I had wished to meet Alice Milligan ... I had followed your work and writings and many an inspiration I caught from your poems and essays.

Alice's reputation, skills and quality of service brought her to the attention of the organising centre of the Gaelic League. In 1906 she had the honour of being nominated to the Coiste Gno, which was the highest ruling committee of the League.

Unfortunately domestic circumstances were beginning to intrude upon her life again and with a certain foreboding, Alice turned down the nomination. She would have loved to have accepted and the Gaelic League would have benefited enormously from her talents exercised at that high level. She was now forty years old, still fit and active and, according to herself, with not a grey hair yet threaded amongst the red.

But Mrs. Milligan's health problems, stemming from an increasingly weak heart, were becoming a pressing worry. The marriages of Charlotte and Edith in 1892 had heralded the beginning of the end of the close and crowded Milligan family life. Gradually they all scattered and built lives of their own.

In 1905, at the age of 17, her youngest brother Charles followed his father into business in the Bank Buildings, Belfast. Ernest gained his primary degree in 1906 and after qualifying as a medical doctor he followed others of his family to England, in search of employment.

Despite the large family circle, Alice was rapidly being manoeuvred into that common fate, that of the unmarried daughter left to look after aging parents.

She told the League that she could not serve it much longer, but that she was ready and willing to train a successor. She continued to work whenever she could. In the winter of 1906-07 she gave a lecture on aspects of Irish history at Kilskeery, Co Tyrone. From 1907, however, her contributions were more and more sporadic as she became confined to the villa "Eastward", in Bangor.

In March 1909, in a letter to Mary Ann Hutton, scholar and Irish patriot, Alice gives some indication of her circumstances:

I cannot now leave home for more than a night or so at a time as one brother has married and gone and Charlie is away from home too so except sisters come over on visits there is no family except myself... I have been a good deal tied up here and out of things.- to even think of you going to Donegal makes me homesick .... my Irish is so rusty.

In September of the same year T.W. Rolleston wrote in reply to a letter from her:

... very sorry to hear of all your trouble about relatives illnesses.

She filled her time with writing and fulfilling any commitments which came her way within reach of home. For example in 1909 she was one of the judges at the   Belfast Feis Costume Competition.   On this

Charlotte Milligan, Alice's mother, in frail old age.

occasion she dressed carefully for the part, making sure to wear Irish material. She wore a brown poplin blouse and a skirt of Douglas Mills tweed, topped by a long overcoat of the same tweed.

She kept up her work for the Irish Folk Song Society and in the spring of 1910 her sister Charlotte came over from London for a visit. It was during this visit that Alice and Charlotte travelled to Omagh to hear and record the traditional singing of brother and sister Éamon and Anne Tracey of Benefreachan. Alice's own account of this visit has already been alluded to briefly (page 17). It is plain that the sisters enjoyed the nostalgia of the joint visit. The coach driver took them on a roundabout route so that they could revisit some of their favourite haunts.

They were entertained all evening by the Tracey's singing in the parlour of The White Hart Hotel where their parents had met fifty years before. Next day they went by train to Trillick for a two day visit on the invitation of Rev. Matthew Maguire, P.P. Charlotte recalled:

On our first evening Father Maguire took us to visit a nightschool held at a place called Knocknagar, where a cabin on the verge of a bog has hitherto done duty for a school. On the second evening of our visit Father Maguire brought us to see a class in one of his well-built and equipped schools which stands, with its experimental garden plot, at the end of the village of Trillick.

On their return to Omagh Charlotte visited the Loreto Convent school before returning to Belfast by train. Alice was taken by Rev. Mons. O'Doherty to see the Irish class at the Girls' National School. She did not immediately follow her sister back to Belfast; instead she took the opportunity to visit her mother's relatives, where she stayed for some days reminiscing about childhood. Her poem 'A Harvester' probably dates from this visit.

The following year, 1911, Charlotte went to the United States on a lecturing tour. This coincided with the publication of her book *Annals of the Irish Harpers*, based on the papers of the musician and antiquary Edward Bunting.

About 1914 Alice's brother William, an officer in the British Army, returned from Chicago. William had literary aspirations himself and in the same year a large novel about the founding of Dublin was published under the authorship of W.H. and Alice Milligan. The review in *The Irish Book Lover* of June 1914 is favourable noticeably giving most of the credit to Alice, who, it says, has been "ably aided by her brother".

When the First World War began, William was called up again on Foreign Service.

Thomas McDonagh — one of the leaders of the 1916 Rising, commander of forces at Jacob's Factory, signatory of the Proclamation of the Republic — was one of Alice's friends. He was also a great admirer of her poetry. Just how highly he regarded her was made plain in an article he wrote for *The Irish Review* of July/August 1914. He had undertaken to contribute a series on living Irish poets. He would like, he said, to begin with the best. His tribute to Alice in this article is based on personal knowledge of his subject:

I know her personally: a few of the poems in her book *Hero Lays* have references to experiences that I shared with her. I have heard her speak of her poems, and know the frank sincerity with which she regards them. I have heard her read them, and know that the harmony of them, their splendid rhythm and their rich music, must be in her immortal soul; for she ruins it sometimes in reading.

McDonagh makes a point which was often made by those who knew her. Alice was entirely:

... without thought of herself, with thought always of Ireland's cause — Alice Milligan is the most Irish of living Irish poets, and therefore the best.

At the end of his article McDonagh makes the startling claim that while she is like Thomas Davis in being primarily a propagandist, "she is a finer poet, with a far better command of word and phrase".

This very public, very high praise marks an apex, perhaps the pinnacle of Alice's reputation. It illustrates also that, regardless of how many letters, lectures, plays and articles she wrote, she was best known to the Irish people, and loved by them, as a poet. She was, says McDonagh, the personification of courage.

Alice was now approaching her fiftieth year, and a cataclysmic year it was to be. But a further strand must be woven into any account of the previous years before the effects of 1916 can be fully appreciated.

Despite their mutual friendship with Francis Joseph

Biggar of "Ardrigh" in Belfast, by Alice's own account she did not meet Roger Casement until June 1904 at a Feis at Waterfoot, near Glenariff on the Co Antrim coast. She had been in Kerry at a hurling match and after a stopover in Belfast, bought a day rail ticket to the Feis, intending to return to Belfast that evening. Amongst the throng at the Feis she met friends who had taken a cottage for some days nearby. They invited Alice to stay with them and it was by taking up this invitation that Alice and Roger Casement met. Each rapidly developed a respect for the other's opinions and abilities.

Just after Casement's execution Alice wrote an article for the *Catholic Bulletin*, October 1916. She recalled:

In the winter following my first meeting with him, he organised a series of five lecture entertainments for me along the Antrim coast and I vividly recall how we drove past the foot of Glenariff, the scene of that delightful summer Feis, in a snowy blast which swept down from the mountain heights. Just as we passed under the Sandstone Arch at Red Bay, the Irish travelling teacher of the district rode by us on his bicycle, and we could scarcely hear the greeting he shouted to us for the roaring of wind and sea. The house of a kinswoman and friend of his was our headquarters, and there we had talk until late in the nights about how the cause of Ireland might best be served and the old tongue revived.

This meeting with the Irish travelling teacher is related in the poem 'The Man on the Wheel'.

Alice went on to recall various acts of kindness

and generosity by Casement which she had witnessed; everyday acts of a simplicity which his heart-
broken friends later remembered. Some examples
include how, at a social gathering, he went out of his
way to carry in chairs high above his head for ladies
who were without seats; how he searched for a wrap
for a lady singer who was about to leave a heated
room; how he took pains to find the times of trains
for any traveller who lacked the information.

On one occasion, as he and Alice walked towards
the Feis sportsfield at Toomebridge, Casement left
her to go down on his knees beside a drunkard to
loosen his collar and move him into the shade.

Alice was also with him the day his knighthood
was announced in 1911:

He was with us in Belfast at one of our big meetings
during the agitation for Irish at the University and once
later at The Ulster Hall. I entered somewhat late, being
detained by a thunderstorm, and I well recollect how he
rose and waved to tell me that there was a vacant seat
beside him. He wore black glasses, and was somewhat
altered and older looking, having just come back from
Putomayo. 'I wouldn't go on the platform,' he whispered,
'someone would have referred to it, you know'.

In old age Alice recounted to a friend how she and
Roger Casement — two years her senior — had taken
a walk round Larne harbour in the spring of 1914. It
was just after the April night when the Unionist Ulster Volunteer Force had landed 35,000 rifles and
five million rounds of ammunition at the port and
distributed them by car to every corner of Ulster in a

highly organised gun-running operation. As they viewed the scene Casement turned to Alice and said: "We'll have to do something like this."

There is little reason to doubt, from evidence both before and after his death, that Alice had a great affection for Roger Casement. Although he spent long and distinguished periods abroad on Consular Service, she knew him only in an Irish context and in Ireland very many people viewed him with respect and affection. Whether there was any more depth to Alice's attachment compared to that of others, is a tantalising and unanswerable question.

While Casement was embarking on the course of action which would earn him an eternal place in Irish history books, Alice Milligan's life was slipping past its high point and narrowing in focus to the Bangor house where her father and mother were now very frail. Charlotte, once the plump, happy mistress of a house buzzing with activity, was now so weak that she was confined to a wheelchair. Her handsome young commercial traveller was now nearing eighty and suffering from diabetes.

As 1916 dawned, Alice was nursing her mother through her final days. Word came that her sister Charlotte was also gravely ill at her home in Chepstow Place, London. Despite her own weakness, Mrs. Milligan was distressed for her eldest daughter and asked Alice to go to London to be with her.

This Alice did, but not before finally saying goodbye to her mother who died on 13th January at the age of 72. For the first time since Evelyn's death in 1903, the grave at Drumragh, Omagh, was opened.

Seaton, Alice's father, was devastated. Nevertheless, Alice had to leave him to go to Charlotte's side. On 25th March, Alice's best loved sister died and followed her mother into the grave.

Charlotte Milligan-Fox was much mourned in London as well as at home. She was a well known figure in London, and her house had been a favourite meeting place for many of the capital's distinguished musical and literary figures.

Alice accompanied her sister's body home and found her father in a fatal decline, unable to sustain this double blow. She had little time to come to terms with her own grief before her father died on 6th April.

For a third time that year the grave was opened and Alice watched her father laid to rest where she herself would one day be buried.

In barely three months Alice's world had been shaken at its foundations. For half a century she had a home with loving parents. No matter how far she travelled, no matter how hard she worked, no matter how daring her opinions, she could always go home. This, the stage scenery of her life, had now vanished. Coupled with that, she had to contend with her grief and sense of bewildered loss without the supportive sharing of suffering with her closest sister for she had to grieve for her also.

Alice had received an emotional battering, but 1916 was not finished with her yet.

About a fortnight after their father's funeral Charles telephoned his sister to tell her there had been a Rising in Dublin. Alice knew nothing about the imminence of the Rising. It came as a total surprise to her. Her personal circumstances at the time must not be forgotten. She was in a state of deep mourning. She had been nursing her parents for a long time. For most of February and March 1916 she was in London for her sister's final weeks, therefore not only out of touch but out of the country.

What is certain is that she shared the shock widely felt as the British government systematically shot the fifteen leaders of the Rising during the month of May. James Connolly was so badly wounded in the fighting that he was unable to stand. He was simply tied into a chair and then shot.

The names of those who died, like Pearse and Clarke, are a matter of history. One of those executed was Thomas McDonagh, the same man who had given Alice such commendation as "the best living Irish poet". A British soldier was reported as saying "They all died well, but McDonagh died like a prince".

Despite her own mourning, Alice took on a role which she was to fulfil many times in the coming years. She became a prison visitor. In her poem 'Arbour Hill, May 1916' she describes a visit to the prison where soldiers were at first embarrassed when they saw her mourning dress, thinking she was a relative of one of the executed rebels. She was merely seeking news of a prisoner for his distraught mother in Belfast who had not heard of him since Easter.

Her heart went out to these men. Whatever her views on the wisdom and timing of the Rising she, like many, regarded the executed leaders as martyrs, and the many men imprisoned as heroes for their country.

Yet another burden was laid upon Alice. News came that her friend Roger Casement had been arrested and waited to stand trial in London for High Treason.

Ironically, Casement had followed the shipment of arms from Germany desperately hoping to persuade the leaders of the Rising that to stage a rebellion now would be the height of folly.

He was put off the submarine on which he travelled, in a canvas canoe in Tralee Bay. The seas were heavy and the canoe overturned. Casement and two companions were lucky to reach shore at Banna Strand. The overturned canoe was found, Casement arrested and transported to London in the salt-stiffened clothes which his captors left to dry on him.

Like many friends and sympathisers, Alice followed him to London, determined to help in any way she could, if only by being there. She haunted the houses of sympathisers and attended the trial every day, rewarded when Casement spotted her and waved across the courtroom. He sent an ironic message to her via his council: " Write a poem about *this*, Alice!"

Her main companion at the trial was the historian Alice Stopford Green who was a close friend of Casement and who, unlike Alice Milligan, was given permission to visit him in Pentonville Prison once a week.

Supporters staged an energetic campaign for clemency but feeling in Britain was running fiercely against Casement. Some idea of the feeling in the country can be gained by an exchange which took place in the British Parliament after Casement's arrest. Mr. Pemberton Billing (Independent) asked the Prime Minister if Sir Roger Casement had been brought to London, and whether he could give the House and the country the assurance that the traitor would be shot forthwith. Prime Minister Asquith replied that he did not think the question ought to be put.

Casement was stripped of his knighthood and strongly criticised for his collaboration with Germany when Britain was at war. The case against him was strong and became even more emotionally charged when the infamous 'black diaries' came to light. These diaries were allegedly Casement's own and chronicled in great detail his secret life as a homosexual. The argument about their authenticity is still alive.

Despite the adverse publicity — some of it very distasteful — Alice's loyalty to Casement never wavered. After Casement had made his famous speech from the dock (during which the judge feigned sleep) and the death sentence was passed, he walked very proudly from the court and Alice never saw him again.

Her poem 'The Ash Tree of Uisneach' was written with the trial as background. She gives clear indication of her feelings about the trial in this poem which was dedicated to Alice Stopford Green. She likened those in the courtroom to an audience at a Roman gladiatorial show, waiting for blood. The drowsy judge gets a mention.

Casement wrote several letters from prison and in

one of these he sent his love to Alice Milligan. On the day of the execution, 3rd August 1916, a crowd gathered outside Pentonville Prison and Alice was amongst them. When the bell tolled to indicate that Casement was dead a tremendous cheer went up from the crowd. It was so loud that it reverberated through the prison corridors.

It was a sound that sickened Alice and which she never forgot. She wrote a poem called 'In the Wirral' for Ita McNeill, another nationalist friend who had been in London for the trial. Ita returned to Ireland the day after the execution while Alice stayed on in England. In this poem, after speaking of 'gay, blood-guilty London' she praises the English countryside and cries:

> How from England's beauty
> Can I my heart withhold?
> By thinking of her crowds that cheered
> When a death bell tolled;
> And the mountains of Wales there,
> For all they look so kind,
> Guard many an Irish mother's son
> Whom I have much in mind.

The fact that Casement's remains were buried in England against his express wishes remained a festering sore. Alice did not live to see Harold Wilson's government give permission for his body to be exhumed and shipped to Ireland where it was re-interred at Glasnevin, Dublin, in March 1965.

The personal and national events of 1916 left Alice Milligan drained and weakened. The pencil drawing of her (the frontispiece of this book) by the eminent Irish artist Sean O'Sullivan, although drawn as late as 1942, shows a woman much altered by experience. The energy, idealism and optimism that had inhabited her was largely snuffed out. She had discovered bitterly that the death of friends is very different from the legends of martyrs. When the harsh realities of friends dying for their country are brought brutally home, the fine, gallant, poetic theory of it is left somewhat wanting.

The day of Casement's execution became one of the most important anniversaries in Alice's year. For the rest of her long life, every 3rd August, in a gesture reminiscent of her memorial to Marjorie Arthur, she gathered flowers and placed them on the mantelpiece where ever she happened to be, in his memory. She would spend that day quietly, remembering and praying.

She still had her aspirations for Ireland. Her hostile attitude to the British government was now laced with a more personal flavour.

It was a bitter fact, however, that the complexities of the Irish nation and the violent politics which were now overtaking it, created a landscape which was becoming strange to her, a turmoil which was leaving her on the sidelines, homeless and bewildered.

A Prisoner and Distressed

For some time, Alice remained in England, staying in the Wirral. Across the estuary of the river Dee she could gaze at the mountains of north Wales. Deep in these mountains at Frongoch was a prison camp where many Irish prisoners were held. Inevitably she made her way there and her poem 'The Shining Dish' recaptures her visit to these men. In the last verse she gives a clear indication of how deeply the national events of the past year had affected her. She had spent decades immortalizing Celtic legend and exhorting contemporary Ireland to learn from her heroes. Now, at the gates of Frongoch:

> Such was the thought that came to me,
> These new times shame the ancient tales.

In one week of war, she said, these men had outdone the mighty Cuchulainn himself.

By the end of 1917 Alice was back in Ireland. She travelled around visiting and staying with friends. She made trips to the Dublin prisons, sent by anxious families in Belfast who had lost contact with their sons and fathers. To these prisoners she became a familiar and welcome figure.

Short snapshot poems survive from this period, such as 'In the Zoo', 'A Boy at the Railings', 'Girls from the Pine Forest'. Her creative energy now concentrated on catching in words brief moments of experience which add up to a very individual and vivid preservation of a country in turmoil.

Her defiant nationalism is still evident, but it is now a bruised emotion.

In 1919 she returned to England to stay with her brother Ernest, now a doctor in Bath, Somerset, and his wife and family of three little daughters. William had left the army at the end of the First World War and was also living with Ernest. One of Ernest's daughters still has five beautiful plates which Alice brought with her as a present for Ernest's wife. Alice had bought a set of six but dropped one on the platform at Crewe Station.

Although Alice may not have fully realized it, this return to England was a tacit renunciation of her independence. She was now fifty-three years old, unmarried with no steady income and with no family property in which she could live.

For someone of her convictions and of her significant experience and renown, it was not a totally happy arrangement. Her brothers were quite unsympathetic and one gains the impression that they were not wholly aware of the status their sister had attained in Ireland or of the nature of her talents and achievements over the previous thirty years. They cannot be entirely blamed for this. One had viewed events from England and the other had been in America and lately away fighting a British war.

Several years later, writing to Mrs. de Valera Alice says, in a tone quite lacking in self-pity:

Since the opening of 1919 I have been more or less of a prisoner, entirely secluded by circumstances amongst relatives entirely opposed to the Republican cause.

Ernest and William still retained the family interest in dreams and the unexplained. When Alice reached them in 1919 they were experimenting with automatic writing. Undoubtedly Alice took seriously any 'messages' which appeared to come from dreams or other supernatural means. Perhaps this is not surprising, given her strong sense of identification with the dead.

She did have her scruples and in the same letter to Mrs. de Valera she strongly emphasised that she had never witnessed a spiritualist seance or:

...sought consultation with a medium - Messages come to me generally from the very relatives who seek to restrain me and detach me from the Irish movement.

For some reason — perhaps the arrangements in Bath proved too awkward or perhaps William was unable to gain employment in England — William and Alice returned to live in Dublin in 1920. William was not finding it easy to settle into civilian life. He was rapidly developing a dependence on alcohol, a state of affairs which distressed Alice who had little experience in dealing with such a problem.

Brother and sister, thrown together by events, intended to set up home together. William needed someone to look after him and, as with her parents, Alice seemed the obvious choice.

This most undomesticated of women found herself once again a prisoner of domesticity.

Douglas Hyde wrote to her with mild surprise in

March 1920:

Fancy your having turned domesticated and deserting the jails now that you are wanted so much there!

1920 was an inauspicious time to have chosen to return. Dublin was in the grip of a vicious struggle between the I.R.A. and the British Army. William and Alice were living in a flat in Kildare Street. His British military connections can have been no secret and his concern for his own safety proved well founded when the I.R.A. gave him twenty-four hours to leave. If he did not, he would be shot.

Why were they so considerate? It is speculative but not unreasonable to wonder if Captain W.H. Milligan may have owed the courtesy of that twenty-four hours, and thereby his life, to the fact that his sister was Alice Milligan, well known by repute for her patriotic work.

The ex-British Army Captain and the renowned Irish patriot hastily bundled up their belongings and fled. Almost certainly they went first to Belfast where their sister Edith lived with her solicitor husband. Alice's letters reveal that she took two hasty visits to Dublin during the crisis surrounding the signing of the Treaty in early 1922.

William worried about his sister's visits to Dublin, not unnaturally after their previous exit. He tried to discourage her by relating dreams of violent disturbances, masonry falling on crowds in the capital. But Alice could not keep away from the action if she could possibly be near it. On the morning of the ratification of the Treaty with Britain, on 7th January

1922, she put on her hat and coat, left William and his dire warnings behind in Belfast and bought a day-return for Dublin.

This Treaty, incidentally, granted universal suffrage to all adults, male and female over the age of 21 in the Free State. This reflected the aspirations of the 1916 Proclamation which explicitly addressed Irishmen *and* Irishwomen and guaranteed "... equal rights and equal opportunities to all its citizens .... cherishing all the children of the nation equally."

The Free State thus preceded Britain by six years in enfranchising all its female citizens.

Five months after the signing the two sides resorted to arms and Civil War broke out.

The Civil War deeply upset Alice. This was not how the consummation of the grand ideal had been envisaged by her fellow enthusiasts. It had all gone horribly wrong. England had been the enemy in ballad and song. Now Irishmen were killing each other. As always, Alice drew on her vast knowledge of Celtic legend and, as was her habit, sought for parallels with the present day.

She found it in the story of Cuchulainn's fight with Ferdia. These two blood brothers were tricked by Queen Maeve of Connaught into fighting each other to the death. She took up her pen and wrote one of her last poems, entitled 'Till Ferdia Came'. An admirer of her work remarked that this poem was the only good thing to have come out of the Civil War.

It is an outpouring of grief for the days that had come. Alice realized the horror of fighting when friend was pitched against former friend and the enemy was no longer an impersonal, historic tyrant.

As Cuchulainn held the dying Ferdia he cried out:

> Oh, battle was a gladsome game
> Till to the ford Ferdia came!

The Ireland that she loved was being torn crazily apart:

> Oh, grief! of griefs beyond all other,
> Two valiant sons of one fond mother...
> ...Oh brothers! Sons of one loved land,
> Who to such combat armed each hand,
> What cause of fury and of hate
> Had either?

The poem ends on a note of almost pathetic optimism:

> As it was then, it may be so
> In these sad days of blood and tears.
> Have faith - trust God for happier years,
> For strength upheld, for peace restored
> 'Twixt those who battle at the ford.

Despite her abhorrence of what was happening, she was unable to keep her opinions neutral. She recounted in a letter to Éamon de Valera's wife a dream which she had some time previously:

...I saw de Valera standing very stern and resolute - he reached out his hand and I clasped it saying 'You will not draw back. You will not yield one inch.' That a split was imminent I did not then foresee.

Now, she felt that this dream justified her instinctive sympathy with de Valera in his Republican stance against those who wished to sign the Treaty with Britain. As she said to Mrs. de Valera:

I understood that in the imminent division I was to belong to Éamon de Valera.

In September 1922 Alice's sister Edith died in Belfast. Edith had herself written a few lyrics for some of Charlotte's Irish music. During the war she had given tireless service particularly in the hospitals. For this work she was awarded a C.B.E. Alice and Edith were never very close — Alice described her as a 'rabid imperialist'.

The once boisterous family circle had shrunk by one more. Of thirteen children, only Charles, the youngest, had a permanent home in Ireland. This was in Bangor which was in the newly created state of Northern Ireland, set up in June 1921. This, together with the Civil War raging in the South, made an unrecognisable travesty of Alice's Ireland.

She and William returned to England and the comparative tranquillity of Ernest's family. An arrangement was made whereby Alice would act as a companion and governess to Ernest's three daughters. Aunt Alice was to become a very happy memory to these three. They remember her for her kindness and gentleness, and how the suffering of children or animals could reduce her to tears.

She would take her nieces for walks and they loved her company. Often she would wear a beautiful reversible emerald satin and black cape which had come from the Abbey Theatre in Dublin.

But events in Ireland had disturbed Alice badly. It was an uncertain time for those, like Alice, who had been vociferous and active in pursuit of their aims. She was from Northern Ireland; her native county, Tyrone, was caught, as she saw it, on the 'wrong' side of the border. Many people with views similar to her own were arrested and questioned.

She reacted in two ways. On the one hand she was relieved to be in England and away from the scene. She wrote to Bulmer Hobson from Bath:

We are most comfortably settled here and much as I regret leaving Ireland I'm sorry I did not come long ago.

Coming from Alice these are surprising words. Perhaps she wanted to retreat, just to leave it all behind and try to recapture a normal family life; a life such as she enjoyed in her girlhood before the 1890's. She gives every impression at this time of being politically and patriotically worn out.

Conversely, her past would not leave her entirely alone. When taking her nieces for walks she would glance round nervously. Sometimes she would go so far as to hustle them quickly into a doorway where she would make them hide saying "Keep in, we are being followed!"

The authorities kept a check on her post and the little girls would hear their parents commenting 'Alice's letters are being opened again'. From some points of view this measure may have been understandable, but it was an irritation which Alice had to learn to live with.

William was writing for the *Boy's Own Paper* and published *Helgi the High Born,* a novel based on the Icelandic Sagas, in 1927. He had married but his wife had left him taking their young son Edward with her. The estrangement was probably caused by William's drinking bouts. The household had to grow accustomed to Uncle William, having had all his money stolen, being returned home by a policeman.

Despite this, he and Alice collaborated on another novel, *The Dynamite Drummer.* Alice's old friend Bulmer Hobson, now one of the directors of publishers Martin Lester, Ltd., of Harcourt Street, Dublin, published it. It is a humorous and satirical work about a naive American who arrives in Northern Ireland and gets into all sorts of trouble with the natives.

This book caused Alice much heartache and many letters to and from Hobson. It was proposed to illustrate the book with a picture of a tipsy Orangeman. William objected and Alice wrote to Hobson that her brother felt that such a picture would not help sell the book in the North. Please could they have a marching Orangeman instead?

After publication sales did not go well. Alice pestered Hobson — have reviews appeared? Is he sure he sent out review copies?

Finally Hobson wrote with the bad news that only 400 copies had been sold. Alice wrote back:

Dear Bulmer,

    I took the liberty of not giving Willy your letter as he is inclined to be deeply depressed just now and would ask you as a great favour to write again to him conveying the same information somewhat differently.

She then goes on to suggest how it could be phrased. She has taken on completely the role of carer for her brother.

After nearly ten years in England Alice and William returned to Ireland. Ernest's children would have outgrown their need for a governess and William's drinking bouts were upsetting to the household. Perhaps also Alice had at last been away from Ireland for long enough. Love of the country was in her bones. She was sixty-six years old. It was time to go back.

After some temporary lodgings in Belfast William obtained a job as an official of the Works Department of the Ministry of Finance for Northern Ireland, based in Omagh, where both he and Alice had been born. Property in Omagh itself was too expensive for them, so they set up house together in The Rectory of the village of Mountfield. Some time later, William's wife Maud and their son rejoined them.

Money was a continual worry and Alice appears, strangely, to have been the only one who tried to keep any account of it. Some royalties were due on the meagre sales of *Dynamite Drummer* but Alice wrote to Bulmer Hobson.

Don't send Willy any royalty money just at present....We are expecting his wife over and I don't want him to spend his resources before she arrives.

On the same subject she wrote again:

I'd almost rather keep him penniless for a week or two, as he has just steadied up and got into his job.

Alice, out of her own tiny resources, mainly from the odd newspaper article or radio broadcast, was supporting him when his own pay packet disappeared. She confided in Hobson:

I have been through a time of intense trouble and anxiety — his wife was more of a disturbing element than a help and will, I fear, continue so.

Maud was apparently a trial to live with. Alice's innate loyalty and dedication were now fully employed in serving this household. Despite his fierce anti-Irish views, she was very fond of her nephew Edward, describing him as marvellously talented and charming.

Occasionally subterfuge was needed in dealing with finance. She cautioned Hobson on one occasion:

Do not write as if you had heard separately from me... When you send the cash — send a receipt for us to sign jointly.

The constraints and stresses on her life in her encroaching old age were onerous. She longed for face to face contact with old friends. On one occasion she contrived to arrange a meeting with Hobson. William's condition nearly denied her this pleasure:

I am so anxious for a solitary talk with you. My brother almost had a relapse Sunday and Monday and I was greatly distressed at prospect of upset of plans.

Her independence had so vanished, and her sur-roundings were so unsympathetic that she was for-bidden to bring any Irish papers into the house. Those whom she now served were thoroughly anti-Irish.

An elderly George Russell, not long before his own death, was so concerned about her that he sent a friend and admirer, Joseph McGarrity, to visit her in Mountfield. This thrilled her immensely. She told him in words laden with nostalgia that his visit was an event in her life which linked her back to the cause for which she lived.

She had to resort to the help of friends in commu-nicating by letter. A sympathiser with an address in High Street, Omagh, wrote to McGarrity:

Perhaps you are not aware that Miss Milligan holds different political views to other members of her family and in consequence it would be better to communicate with me at the above address.

In August 1933, after an absence of ten years, she managed one visit to Dublin for a meeting of the Yeats Academy. She relished the contact with old comrades. She stayed in the home of Mrs. Kent, widow of Thomas Kent, one of the fifteen executed leaders of the Easter Rising. She also visited Gavan Duffy, the solicitor who had prepared the defence for Roger Casement. They were the owners of a portrait of Casement which was the last photograph taken of him in Germany.

There was more trouble ahead. On March 11th 1934, Alice's nephew Edward suffered a stroke. He was only twenty-six. He could not speak or stand and needed round the clock nursing. On being notified by the local doctor, his uncle Ernest came over from England and ensured that Edward received the most modern treatment available.

Edward's speech returned and his spirits lifted. It was a temporary respite for pneumonia set in and he died on May 3rd.

It was now a sad and elderly household. The water pipes in the Rectory were made of lead and William always maintained that this had an effect on his son, causing the stroke. Nor did he feel it was doing himself any good as he was suffering repeated bouts of illness. His wife Maud was now a most difficult invalid. Alice coped with them both, and the ever present severe money worries.

Finally, on 26th June 1937, William died, aged sixty five.

Alice's brothers, Seaton (now retired in California), Charles (in Bangor), and Ernest (now in Glossop, Derbyshire) exchanged correspondence on what to do about Alice. She was now seventy-one years old, virtually destitute and with a difficult, invalid sister-in-law to care for. In Mountfield a collection was organised for her and £272 pounds were raised. William's car was sold to a neighbouring farmer.

Despite her efforts to keep solvent Alice wrote to Ernest with reluctance to ask for help in settling the half-year's rent. Ernest told Charles who immediately contacted her to say he also would help her in any way he could.

Alice was very annoyed. She had told Ernest that she did not wish for help from Charles because of his own family commitments. She sold many items from her book collection, as well as old prints in her possession. Maud had a cousin in England who sent her clothes, and occasionally included something for Alice. Writing still occupied her but now her motive was largely to bring in some income. She was interviewed by both the B.B.C. and R.T.E. as something of an historical curiosity.

Seaton had only a few months in which to consider his sister's predicament for he himself died in November of the same year, 1937, aged 68. It had been many, many years since Alice had seen him, once her best loved brother and companion of many outings and intrigues in happy younger days.

Despite her circumstances Alice showed that although it might burn low, the old fire was not extinguished. When a leaflet was issued by the Northern Council for Unity in January 1938 entitled 'Partition of Ireland: the root of DISCONTENT, DISORDER AND DISTRESS', she was one of sixteen signatories from all over Northern Ireland. She was also the only woman of the sixteen.

In 1939 Yeats died. Alice's admiration for Yeats had diminished somewhat over the years. Their audiences were too different, and perhaps Alice did not think his motives in writing were as pure as her own. She wrote only for Ireland; he wrote also for fame.

John O'Leary, Alice's old friend, had died in 1907.

Alice aged about
seventy six

His active campaigning days were in the middle of the nineteenth century. He used to share with Alice his feeling of loneliness and futility as the years passed and he outlived all his contemporaries and the Irish stage passed on to scenes he found unfamiliar.

Alice remembered him now as she faced the same fate. An old friend in Cork wrote to her:

Your letter came to me like a pleasant breeze from the old campaigning days of the Language Movement. We all remember when you travelled the length and breadth of Ireland with a magic lantern and tableaux of Irish history. I myself remember Ethna Carbery and yourself at the Oireachtas [the Gaelic League's annual congress] in the early days, when it was grand to be alive and everybody was so enthusiastic. How different things are today!

Maud in her turn died and for some time Alice lived alone with her memories and her cats — of which she had several. She would sit on a garden bench at the back of the house, talking to them and grooming them. But she was well into her seventies and becoming less able to look after herself. During the second World War she finally left Mountfield, going to stay with friends at Kells, Co Antrim. Here two sisters and a brother maintained a small farm.

The country proved it had not entirely forgotten her when, in 1941, the National University of Ireland conferred the Honorary Doctor of Literature upon her. This gave her great pleasure. It was very late recognition, but nevertheless, to the new Dr. Alice Milligan it was some comfort to know that there were those who had not entirely overlooked her life's work.

The honour did little to help her financial circumstances. The poverty of her declining years is one of the most saddening aspects of her life. Given the course that her life took it was almost inevitable, as this paragraph from an "Alice Milligan Testimonial" issued in 1942, shows:

While she is still alive we think something should be done to show our appreciation of her work. We feel there is a more definite obligation on us of making to her some return, however slight, for a lifetime's work that brought no income, no royalties, but left her much poorer in worldly goods.

Originally the group which circulated this Testimonial hoped to publish a selection of her poems but found the difficulty of collecting them prohibitive. The Testimonial explains:

Miss Milligan has been writing for over fifty years and

has kept no copies of her work, nor even records of time and place of publication, so indifferent was she to self-interest.

Instead subscriptions were gathered and at the Tyrone Feis held in Omagh in 1943 a Reception was given for her at which she was presented with a cheque. One of the local newspapers, *The Ulster Herald*, reported the speaker as saying:

Today we have the honour to present her with a cheque subscribed to by the President, the Cardinal Primate, leaders of the Church and State, and by persons of humble rank, by Protestants and Catholics, by people from every province of Ireland.

The speaker admitted that the sum should be greater but that the younger generation in Ireland quite simply did not know who she was. Not for the first time the hope was expressed that her poems would be reprinted.

After some years living in Kells, one of the sisters died. Circumstances became more and more difficult as gradually it became clear that no-one in the house was able to care properly for the others. One visitor to Alice in those years remembers seeing her out in the lane with a shovel trying to fill in potholes with gravel. She was at least eighty years old.

In 1950 the publishers M.H. Gill and Son, Ltd. of Dublin gathered together and published some of the poetry of that literary trio of long ago, Ethna Carbery, Seumas McManus and Alice Milligan. This was the last time Alice saw her work in print. The volume was entitled *We Sang for Ireland*. The tense used in the title underscores the feeling that their words were for the previous generation and that the publication is a gesture to nostalgia.

Charles had become very concerned about his sister and, in discussion with him, Alice said that she would very much like to end her days in Tyrone, as near to Omagh, her birthplace, as possible.

Charles made enquiries in Omagh and, with the willing help of the local priest, Father P. McLoingsigh, a home was found for Alice in the townland of Tyrcur, about five miles north of the town. A widowed lady, Mrs. McSwiggan and her two unmarried daughters took her in, in June 1951.

It proved to be a happy arrangement. Mrs. McSwiggan cared for her diligently as she became more infirm.

Occasionally she might take a short walk along the roads nearby, but the whirlwind energy had entirely vanished. Her eyesight deteriorated to the extent that she used a magnifying glass to read.

Relatives and friends visited her and Charles paid for a taxi firm to take her where ever she wished to go. Ernest came over from England to see her for the last time. Charles visited frequently, able at that time to go by train from Bangor to Omagh.

The McSwiggans were struck, as many had been who met her, by her gentle kindness, a characteristic not always evident in her public persona of fifty years previously.

Mrs. McSwiggan had a white turkey which took ill and Alice nursed it back to health. When Christmas came, she would not hear of its being killed. "Oh, no," she said "I couldn't eat a friend".

In contrast, she had developed the fearless, forthright dogmatism so often manifested in the old age of strong-minded people. The Methodist minister came to visit her. She barked "Who are you?" in Irish. When this was translated the minister replied, no doubt with some trepidation, that his name was Mr. England.

Alice truculently protested that 'England' could not be a proper name, and that it must be an assumed name. Mr. England assured her that it was the name he had come into the world with.

During Easter Week, 1953, Alice listened very intently to the radio for the programmes of reminiscence and commemoration of the Rising. As history was remembered she picked out names of people she had known and who were now just ink in the history books. Once again dreams began to disturb and upset her.

On Sunday 12th April there were friends in the house. Alice spent a happy afternoon talking of old times. Later that evening she went up to bed as usual. When Mrs. McSwiggan checked on her about an hour later, she found Alice in bed but feeling unwell.

As the night wore on Alice's breathing became more laboured and she seemed again to be distressed by sporadic dreams. In the early hours of Monday morning, she died. She was eighty-six.

At last this "darling little electric battery", this "little storehouse of vitality" was able to lay down the burden and rest with all whom she had loved and who had left her alone.

It was thirty seven years since she had stood at the gates of Pentonville and heard the bell toll and the crowds cheer as one of her best friends was hanged.

Maud Gonne outlived Alice by a fortnight.

In death all the lines of sorrow and care fell away and her face took on a smoothness recalling the youth and vigour of the high-spirited redhead who, decades before, had discovered Ireland and dedicated her life to its service.

On Wednesday, 15th April, a small private service was held in the front room of the Tyrcur house. The same Methodist minister, Rev. R.L. England, conducted the service. The funeral was small and as the cortege wound through the rain-swept streets of Omagh, scarcely anyone remarked upon it, as it made its way to the family grave at Drumragh. The mourners stood in the graveyard as light rain fell and the coffin was lowered. They represented relatives and friends from across the whole spectrum of the community.

Messages came from all parts of Ireland, amongst them sympathy from Éamon de Valera and other members of the Irish government. The President of Ireland, Sean T. O'Kelly, sent a message which read:

May I offer through you to all your family my own profound sympathy and that of the people of Ireland on the death of Miss Alice Milligan. Your sister was a most distinguished Irishwoman and devoted her great talent to the cause of Irish Independence and the preservation

of the National Language. Ireland mourns her loss. Ar
deis de go riab a h-anam uasal.

The grave inscription is simple:

ALICE L. MILLIGAN
Nior car fod eile ac Eirinn.
She loved no other place but Ireland.
Born Omagh September 1866
Died Omagh April 1953.

During the next few days obituaries began to appear in the national and local press. One student in
Belfast, reading of her death, was overheard to say:
"Who was this Alice Milligan anyway? Should I
know her?"

Many people, from the famous to the unknown,
had regarded her with respect and affection. But by
the time she died the generation which had loved
and honoured her was dead, and her own ending
was very lonely.

Charles, as he stood by her grave in the rain, may
have been reminded of a poem Alice wrote for him
long ago in the 1890's when he was a little child. It
was called 'A Benediction'. In the third stanza Alice
wrote:

> And I bequeath,
> When I must rest my share of earth beneath,
> My days of toil being done,
> The hope of this so nearly hopeless heart
> To you, weak little one,
> To be cherished and held apart,

Perhaps by failure to be tried and shaken,
Yet not by you forsaken,
But kept, as I have kept it, handed on
Till, when you too are dust beneath the flowers
Triumph at last is ours,
When darkness yields to dawn;
And may it be our best of Heaven to know
That God has made it so.

Alice Milligan may rightly be remembered as a fiery and tireless patriot. One wonders if she ever had the thought that troubled Yeats in his later years as he reviewed his work:

Did that play of mine sent out
Certain men the English shot?
('The Man and the Echo')

Did she ever look back on some of her oratory with unease, and ponder the responsibility of being — again using Yeats' analogy — one of those who helped to wind the clock that struck with such seismic effect?

She was much more than a patriot. She was a unique individual. The caring and selfless nature which so many remembered may have its basis in a belief which she explained in one of her many newspaper articles, this one from 1907:

But it is forgotten that the essential of true patriotism as of true religion is the third of the Christian graces. Faith, hope, love. It is the last which matters most.

Postscript

In the months after Alice's death, those who knew her made attempts to collect her poems. Éamon de Valera, her old friend and the Taoiseach (Prime Minister) at the time was most anxious that her work should be preserved. In a letter to Charles he expressed a desire that her entire output should be preserved in the National Library to ensure its availability to editors who might wish to publish it. He wrote:

...I would request your aid so that your distinguished sister's work may be saved for the nation.

As a result, Henry Mangan selected and edited a volume entitled simply *Poems* which was published by Gill & Son in 1954. This volume of sixtyone of her poems presents her work from girlhood to 'Till Ferdia Came'. While it is an excellent presentation it omits many fine poems — inevitably so because her output was so large.

Reviews of this volume were mainly favourable although one critic commented that there were poems included which the poet herself might have preferred to be forgotten.

Her work is not all of high quality, although when it is good — as in for example 'The Return of Lugh Lamh-Fhada'— it is memorable indeed.

The unevenness of style may be accounted for by the fact that, as Mangan says in his introduction to the book, Alice sometimes did not 'polish' her poems.

Her aim was national revival and her poems were sent out hither and thither to serve that purpose. She did not, as some of her contemporaries did, have a desire to build a literary corpus which would be dissected and admired in time to come.

Her more personal poems, such as those for Marjorie Arthur, are amongst her best. In these she is not trying to impress or exhort, simply to express the thoughts of her heart.

She was not a complicated person. She cannot be psychoanalysed or studied in depth, layer after layer, as Yeats can be. She was always simply herself and wrote with openness and a total lack of guile. Periodicals were a favourite medium for her because through them she could reach the ordinary Irish person who perhaps would not have access to books so readily.

The obscurity which has engulfed her memory is not entirely deserved. Her life story is woven like a vibrant thread through the colourful tapestry that was one of Ireland's most historic and formative periods. She was not one of the giants of the era, but she greatly influenced the landscape across which they marched.

One of her most underestimated achievements was the periodical of the 1890's, the *Shan Van Vocht*. It is rarely mentioned in the history books and yet it was a living link in the chain of events which ran from Parnell to the Easter Rising.

In modern days, her grave has been the object of both hatred and honour. Wreaths have been place beneath her name by one faction; others have tried to chisel away the Irish inscription. At least once explosives were used to try to obliterate her memorial.

What would she make of Ireland now, a century after the zenith of her own achievements?

Perhaps it is good that she did not live to see it.

Bibliography

Belfast and Province of Ulster Directories

Bourke, Marcus *John O'Leary; a study in Irish separatism* Anvil, 1967

Boyd, Ernest *Ireland's Literary Renaissance* Figgis 1968

Boylan, Henry *Dictionary of Irish Biography* Gill and Macmillan 1988

Brown, Terence *Ireland: a Social and Cultural History, 1922 - 1985* Fontana 1985

Collins, M.E. *Ireland Three* Educational Co. 1972

Davis, Richard *Arthur Griffith and non-violent Sinn Fein* Anvil 1974

Feeney, W.J. (ed) *Irish Drama series Vol. 2* de Paul Univ 1967

Foster, R.F. *Modern Ireland 1600 - 1972* Penguin/Allen Lane 1988

Graham, Evelyn *Lord Darling and his famous trials* Hutchinson 1929

Henderson, J.W. & Fry, P.P. *Book of M.C.B.* Methodist College, Belfast 1939

Hogan, Robert *Dictionary of Irish Literature* Gill and Macmillan 1985

Kee, Robert *The Green Flag, Vol. 2: The Bold Fenian Men* Penguin 1989

Lyons, F.S. *Ireland since the famine* Fontana 1973

MacBride, Maud Gonne *A Servant of the Queen* Gollancz 1974

Milligan, Charles *My Bangor, from the 1890's*

Milligan, Charles *Second thoughts in which I recall*

Moody, T.W. & Martin, F.X. (eds) *The Course of Irish history* Mercier 1977

O'Connor, Ulick *A Terrible Beauty is Born: the Irish troubles 1912 - 1922* Hamish Hamilton 1975

O'Hegarty, P.S. *A history of Ireland under the Union, 1801 - 1922* Methuen 1952

O'Hehir, Kathryn *Alice Milligan: the Celtic Twilight's forgotten star* Thesis submitted to the University of North Dakota, 1991. Copy in Irish and Local Studies Library, Omagh

Oram, Hugh *The Newspaper Book: a history of newspapers in Ireland 1649 -1983* Dublin: MO Books 1983

Owens, Rosemary Cullen *Smashing Times: a history of the Irish Women's Suffrage movement 1889 - 1922* Attic 1984

Power, P.C. *The Story of Anglo-Irish poetry 1800 - 1922* Mercier 1967

Sawyer, Roger *Casement: the flawed hero* Routledge 1984

Slater's *Directories*

Weygandt, Cornelius *Irish Plays and Playwrights* New York, Kennikat, 1966

Yeats, W.B. *The Collected Letters, Vol 1, 1865 - 1895* ed. John Kelly, Oxford 1986

Yeats, W.B. *Memoirs* Transcribed and edited by Denis Donoghue. Macmillan 1972

The Northern Patriot and *The Shan Van Vocht* held on microfilm in the Irish Collection, Central Library, Belfast.

A number in **bold** type denotes
an illustration

Index